26131

General editor: Graham Handley MA Ph.D.

Gorseinon College
Learning Resource Centre
Belgrave Road : Gorseinon : Swansea : SA4 6RD   Tel: (01792) 890731
This book is **YOUR RESPONSIBILITY** and is due for return/renewal
on or before the last date shown.

CLASS NO. 822·33 KW   ACC. NO.   26131

RETURN OR RENEW -

D1333569

MACMILLAN

First published by James Brodie Ltd
This revised edition first published 1990
by Pan Books Ltd

Published 1992 by
MACMILLAN PRESS LTD
Houndmills, Basingstoke, Hampshire RG21 6XS
and London
Companies and representatives
throughout the world

ISBN 0–333–58176–8

11 10 9 8 7 6 5
02 01 00 99 98

Printed in Great Britain by
Mackays of Chatham PLC
Chatham, Kent

Contents

Line references in these Notes are to the
Arden Shakespeare: King Lear,
but as references are also given to particular acts
and scenes, the Notes may be used with any
edition of the play.

Preface

This student revision aid is based on the principle that in any close examination of Shakespeare's plays 'the text's the thing'. Seeing a performance, or listening to a tape or record of a performance, is essential and is in itself a valuable and stimulating experience in understanding and appreciation. However, a real evaluation of Shakespeare's greatness, of his universality and of the nature of his literary and dramatic art, can only be achieved by constant application to the texts of the plays themselves. These revised editions of Brodie's Notes are intended to supplement that process through detailed critical commentary.

The first aim of each book is to fix the whole play in the reader's mind by providing a concise summary of the plot, relating it back, where appropriate, to its source or sources. Subsequently the book provides a summary of each scene, followed by *critical comments*. These may convey its importance in the dramatic structure of the play, creation of atmosphere, indication of character development, significance of figurative language etc, and they will also explain or paraphrase difficult words or phrases and identify meaningful references. At the end of each act revision questions are set to test the student's specific and broad understanding and appreciation of the play.

An extended critical commentary follows this scene by scene analysis. This embraces such major elements as characterization, imagery, the use of blank verse and prose, soliloquies and other aspects of the play which the editor considers need close attention. The paramount aim is to send the reader back to the text. The book concludes with a series of revision questions which require a detailed knowledge of the play; the first of these has notes by the editor of what *might* be included in a written answer. The intention is to stimulate and to guide; the whole emphasis of this commentary is to encourage the student's *involvement* in the play, to develop disciplined critical responses and thus promote personal enrichment through the imaginative experience of our greatest writer.

Graham Handley

Shakespeare and the
Elizabethan playhouse

William Shakespeare was born in Stratford-upon-Avon in 1564, and there are reasons to suppose that he came from a relatively prosperous family. He was probably educated at Stratford Grammar School and, at the age of eighteen, married Anne Hathaway, who was twenty-six. They had three children, a girl born shortly after their marriage, followed by twins in 1585 (the boy died in 1596). It seems likely that Shakespeare left for London shortly after a company of visiting players had visited Stratford in 1585, for by 1592 – according to the jealous testimony of one of his fellow-writers Robert Greene – he was certainly making his way both as actor and dramatist. The theatres were closed because of the plague in 1593; when they reopened Shakespeare worked with the Lord Chamberlain's Men, later the King's Men, and became a shareholder in each of the two theatres with which he was most closely associated, the Globe and the Blackfriars. He later purchased New Place, a considerable property in his home town of Stratford, to which he retired in 1611; there he entertained his great contemporary Ben Jonson (1572–1637) and the poet Michael Drayton (1563–1631). An astute businessman, Shakespeare lived comfortably in the town until his death in 1616.

This is a very brief outline of the life of our greatest writer, for little more can be said of him with certainty, though the plays – and poems – are living witness to the wisdom, humanity and many-faceted nature of the man. He was both popular and successful as a dramatist, perhaps less so as an actor. He probably began work as a dramatist in the late 1580s, by collaborating with other playwrights and adapting old plays, and by 1598 Francis Meres was paying tribute to his excellence in both comedy and tragedy. His first original play was probably *Love's Labour's Lost* (1590) and while the theatres were closed during the plague he wrote his narrative poems *Venus and Adonis* (1593) and *The Rape of Lucrece* (1594). The sonnets were almost certainly written in the 1590s though not published until 1609; the first 126 seem to be addressed to a young man who was his friend and patron, while the rest are concerned with the 'dark lady'.

The dating of Shakespeare's plays has exercised scholars ever since the publication of the First Folio (1623), which listed them as comedies, histories and tragedies. It seems more important to look at them chronologically as far as possible, in order to trace Shakespeare's considerable development as a dramatist. The first period, say to the middle of the 1590s, included such plays as *Love's Labour's Lost*, *The Comedy of Errors*, *Richard III*, *The Taming of the Shrew*, *Romeo and Juliet* and *Richard II*. These early plays embrace the categories listed in the First Folio, so that Shakespeare the craftsman is evident in his capacity for variety of subject and treatment. The next phase includes *A Midsummer's Night's Dream*, *The Merchant of Venice*, *Henry IV Parts 1* and *2*, *Henry V* and *Much Ado About Nothing*, as well as *Julius Caesar*, *As You Like It* and *Twelfth Night*. These are followed, in the early years of the 17th century, by his great tragic period: *Hamlet*, *Othello*, *King Lear* and *Macbeth*, with *Antony and Cleopatra* and *Coriolanus* belonging to 1607–09. The final phase embraces the romances (1610–13), *Cymbeline*, *The Tempest* and *The Winter's Tale* and the historical play *Henry VIII*.

Each of these revision aids will place the individual text under examination in the chronology of the remarkable dramatic output that spanned twenty years from the early 1590s to about 1613. The practical theatre for which Shakespeare wrote and acted derived from the inn courtyards in which performances had taken place, the few playhouses in his day being modelled on their structure. They were circular or hexagonal in shape, allowing from the balconies and boxes around the walls full view of the stage. This large stage, which had no scenery, jutted out into the pit, the most extensive part of the theatre, where the poorer people – the 'groundlings' – stood. There was no roof (though the Blackfriars, used from 1608 onwards, was an indoor theatre) and thus bad weather meant no performance. Certain plays were acted at court, and these private performances normally marked some special occasion. Costumes, often rich ones, were used, and music was a common feature, with musicians on or under the stage; this sometimes had additional features, for example a trapdoor to facilitate the entry of a ghost. Women were barred by law from appearing on stage, and all female parts were played by boy actors; this undoubtedly explains the many instances in Shakespeare where a woman has to conceal her identity by disguising

herself as a man, e.g. Rosalind in *As You Like It*, Viola in *Twelfth Night*.

Shakespeare and his contemporaries often adapted their plays from sources in history and literature, extending an incident or a myth or creating a dramatic narrative from known facts. They were always aware of their own audiences, and frequently included topical references, sometimes of a satirical flavour, which would appeal to – and be understood by – the groundlings as well as their wealthier patrons who occupied the boxes. Shakespeare obviously learned much from his fellow dramatists and actors, being on good terms with many of them. Ben Jonson paid generous tribute to him in the lines prefaced to the First Folio of Shakespeare's plays:

Thou art a monument without a tomb,
And art alive still, while thy book doth live
And we have wits to read, and praise to give.

Among his contemporaries were Thomas Kyd (1558–94) and Christopher Marlowe (1564–93). Kyd wrote *The Spanish Tragedy*, the revenge motif here foreshadowing the much more sophisticated treatment evident in *Hamlet*, while Marlowe evolved the 'mighty line' of blank verse, a combination of natural speech and elevated poetry. The quality and variety of Shakespeare's blank verse owes something to the innovatory brilliance of Marlowe but carries the stamp of individuality, richness of association, technical virtuosity and, above all, the genius of imaginative power.

The texts of Shakespeare's plays are still rich sources for scholars, and the editors of these revision aids have used the Arden editions of Shakespeare, which are regarded as pre-eminent for their scholarly approach. They are strongly recommended for advanced students, but other editions, like The New Penguin Shakespeare, The New Swan, The Signet are all good annotated editions currently available. A reading list of selected reliable works on the play being studied is provided at the end of each commentary and students are advised to turn to these as their interest in the play deepens.

Literary terms used in these Notes

A few specialist usages are given below, but where there is a full explanation of a term in either the *Textual notes* or *critical commentary* it is not defined here.

iambic pentameter This is the staple line of English narrative and dramatic poetry. 'Pentameter' indicates that there are five beats, feet or stresses in the line. Iambs are feet in which there is a short syllable followed by a long, or an unstressed followed by a stressed. 'Without' is an iamb, for example.

irony The conveyance of meaning by words whose literal sense is the opposite of that implied.

dramatic irony This occurs when a character is unaware of the true significance of his words or actions but other characters on stage, as well as the reader and the audience, know exactly what is happening.

metaphor This is a figure of speech in which two things are not merely compared (as in a simile) but identified. It is not introduced by 'like' or 'as'.

catharsis A word used by Aristotle to describe the effect of tragedy on the audience. According to the context it can mean either purging or purification.

hubris Another of Aristotle's terms from the *Poetics*, hubris is the kind of blind pride characteristic of the tragic hero.

The play

Plot

Lear, a powerful king declining in years, decides to hand over the kingdom to his three daughters: Goneril (the eldest), Regan, and Cordelia (the youngest and best-loved). He stages a ceremony in which each daughter is asked to declare her love. When Cordelia refuses to exaggerate, she is married to the King of France without a dowry, cut out of the king's will, and effectively banished. Lear, who had intended to live with Cordelia, now announces that he will divide his time between Regan and Goneril, accompanied by his retinue of one hundred knights.

Lear's two elder daughters soon lose their patience with him and his – as they claim – rowdy followers. Each is eager for supreme power and jealous of the other's affections for Edmund, bastard son of the Earl of Gloucester. They both begin to plot for dominance – Regan with her husband's connivance, Goneril without. Meanwhile Lear goes mad from a combination of remorse, humiliation and self-doubt, exacerbated by extreme old age. It is left to Cordelia to bring over an army from France to rescue the king and restore order in the state. However, this army is defeated, the king and his daughter are taken prisoner, and Cordelia is murdered in prison – the final blow which, though he had been restored to sanity, kills the king.

There is a sub-plot involving the Earl of Gloucester, who is tricked by his bastard son Edmund into believing that his legitimate son Edgar is a traitor, and wishes to kill him for his inheritance. Distraught with grief, Gloucester declares Edgar an outlaw, but takes pity on the abandoned Lear, for which he is blinded by Regan and Cornwall. In this they are helped by Edmund, who really is plotting to seize Edgar's inheritance by disposing of his father and brother. Gloucester is eventually saved by the disguised Edgar, but dies of grief and joy when Edgar reveals his identity. Edgar then kills Edmund in single combat, while Goneril, who has poisoned her sister Regan, to secure Edmund for herself, is betrayed by her letter to him and commits suicide.

The essence of both plots is misunderstanding between parents and children, but there is a clear difference between them. Gloucester is tricked by Edmund, whereas Lear deceives himself. Naturally enough Lear's case is treated in far more detail, and there is a greater degree of psychological realism in his portrayal. Gloucester remains, to some extent, an emblematic figure, a secondary Job who throws light on the protagonist's sufferings.

Classical doctrine states that the plot of a tragedy must be unified. *King Lear* violates this law to superb effect. As the German critic A. W. Schlegel put it in his *Lectures on Dramatic Art and Literature* (1811):

> Were Lear alone to suffer from his daughters, the impression would be limited to the powerful compassion felt by us for his private misfortune. But two such unheard-of examples taking place at the same time have the appearance of a great commotion in the moral world: the picture becomes gigantic, and fills us with such alarm as we should entertain at the idea that the heavenly bodies might one day fall from their appointed orbits.

Sources and their treatment

Lear's story was well-known in Tudor times and appears in several different versions among Shakespeare's contemporaries. Edmund Spenser, for example, includes it as part of his history of Britain in *The Faerie Queen*, Book 2 Canto X, where the old king is described as discovering that 'love is not, where most it is profest . . .' having already been told by Cordelia that 'she lov'd him as behov'd . . .'

In Higgins's *The Mirror For Magistrates* the story is set in 800 BC and Cordelia is made to tell her own story, explaining that her refusal to pander to Lear's vanity was a deliberate ploy to expose her sisters' falseness: 'I lov'd you ever as my father well,/No otherwise . . ./Thus much I said, the more their flattery to detect . . .' And in Holinshed's *Chronicles*, often used as a source by Shakespeare, Cordelia tells her father that 'so much as you have, so much you are worth, and/so much I love you and no more . . .'

In all these versions of the story Cordelia commits suicide: in Spenser's account she hangs herself, weary of her life in prison. In the earlier version of the play, which Shakespeare drew on, she does not commit suicide: there is a happy ending, with Regan and Goneril defeated and Lear restored to his throne. *King Leir* (sic) is something of a Cinderella story, in which the old king deliberately sets up the love-test in I, 1 in order to trick Cordella (sic) into marriage, when she declines to marry except for love, whereas her father wants to make a dynastic match with the King of Brittany. Like Shakespeare's version, the play hinges on the daughter's love and the father's perverseness, but Shakespeare has crucially shifted the emphasis from romantic to filial affection, and this immeasurably strengthens the drama. Paradoxically, it does this by playing down the obvious and logical motivations which are clear enough in the earlier *King Leir* i.e. Leir's foreign policy, Cordella's high-principled attitude to marriage. By making the characters more opaque Shakespeare emphasizes the irrational, symbolic level of the play. The archrealist novelist Tolstoy noticed this in his comments on *King Lear*, but drew from it the conclusion that Shakespeare's play was therefore inferior to the earlier version, because it employed 'false effects' and was not 'natural' (see *Tolstoy on Shakespeare*, 1907). But in *King Lear* we can see Shakespeare moving into his last poetic and symbolic phase, the years in which he writes *The Tempest* and *The Winter's Tale*, plays which show little interest in the kind of realism for which Tolstoy himself had such genius.

The two versions of *King Lear* touch at many points, but all Shakespeare's additions and alterations are crucial. He makes the play end with the death of Lear and Cordelia, not their victory, and this helps to change it from a chronicle to a tragedy. He adds the Fool, providing a reflection of, and truthful running commentary on, Lear's progress. He makes Lear mad, which the earlier version does not, thus raising the whole temperature of the drama, and he adds besides the false madness of Edgar, which introduces another dimension of meaning associated with his favourite appearance/reality theme. *King Lear* is not merely a sequence of events but a profound symbolic drama in which fundamental questions of existence are touched on: this is the main respect in which it differs from *King Leir*.

Perhaps the most substantial single addition, however, is the Edmund/Gloucester sub-plot, found in none of the other versions. Just as Shakespeare condensed the first seven scenes of *King Leir* into his own I,1 and changed Cordelia's suicide into her murder, synchronizing it with Lear's own death, so his additions, such as the sub-plot, conduce to dramatic intensity, rather than diffuseness. Everything he does is meant to point to the central situation. The sub-plot does exactly this in a number of ways, both obvious and subtle.

Shakespeare took the idea from Philip Sidney's *Arcadia*, a long and complicated prose romance in which many stories are entangled. Parallels between Lear and Gloucester are clear enough: two elderly fathers betrayed by the children they trust and misjudging the children they most love, who eventually try to save them in spite of this. The two stories are brought together largely through Edmund, one of the play's crucial figures, whose illegitimacy stands for far more than mere bastardy. But the differences are perhaps even more important. To begin with, Lear and Gloucester are very different characters, the one powerful and violent, the other credulous and temporizing. Though neither is bad, neither is wholly good, but Lear's faults stand out, as befits the hero, in greater relief, and his fate is accordingly more heroic. Gloucester, on the other hand, plays a secondary role; and while, in the blinding, he endures a worse physical horror than any of Lear's, the point is that Shakespeare wishes us to concentrate on Lear's *inner* life, his metaphysical struggle. At best Gloucester achieves a stoical resignation to the will of the gods, but Lear is brought to examine that will and what it means. In Gloucester's blinding we see virtue impartially tormented; in Lear's madness the notion of meaning in human life is itself on trial – as the other characters recognize (e.g. V, 3, 263–4).

This is brought home in the working of the two plots. Where Gloucester is easily fooled by the scheming Edmund, Lear brings trouble on himself. Where Cordelia shows herself openly throughout, Edgar conceals his identity until the last moment. Where Edmund is at times almost comic in the insouciance of his plotting, Regan and Goneril are merely vile, and where he repents they follow through their desires to a logical conclusion. All these aspects put the main plot on an altogether grander level than the sub-plot. Beyond this, both Gloucester and Edmund are rational in a sense that Lear and Cordelia are not. Edmund looks to his own advantage and, while he is ready to take risks, calculates them as nearly as he can. Gloucester wants a quiet life and tries to smooth things over. But Lear seems to go looking for trouble, and Cordelia shows a strange obstinacy in refusing to placate her father – strange, that is, if we judge the play in terms of the realistic presentation of motive. But as noticed earlier, the writer stresses the opacity of their characters: in them, the need to love and be loved is an absolute demand, outside the scope of calculation. While all the urges in the play can be seen as irrational in one sense or another, all the other characters at least appear to be measuring up advantages, except for France who expounds the doctrine by which Cordelia and, in the end, Lear, live:

> Love's not love
> When it is mingled with regards that stand
> Aloof from the entire point . . . (I, 1, 237–9)

In the last act Edgar manifests such love for his father, and it breaks Gloucester's heart and kills him. Lear, on the other hand, survives a similar display from Cordelia: it is her death which finishes him. Again plot and sub-plot are contrasted.

Date

In the sequence of great tragedies *King Lear* comes between *Othello* and *Macbeth* and seems to have been written in the winter of 1605. The play draws heavily on Harsnett's *Declaration of Egregious Popish Impostures*, entered in the Stationers' Register (the official list of new publications) in March 1603, and to some extent on an earlier version of the same story, *The True Chronicle History of King Leir*, published in mid 1605.

Scene summaries, critical commentary, textual notes and revision questions

Act I Scene 1

The play opens with a casual conversation between Gloucester and Kent introducing two topics: the imminent division of the kingdom, and Edmund's bastardy. The implicit link made between power and inheritance is immediately taken up on Lear's entry. Having decided to abdicate in favour of his daughters, the old man stages a ceremony in which each is asked to pledge her loyalty by declaring her love in fulsome terms. Regan and Goneril comply and are rewarded; Cordelia, his favourite child, refuses, and is married off to France without a dowry by her furious father, who banishes Kent for trying to intercede on her behalf. Cordelia's share is divided between Regan and Goneril, who are to receive their father and his retinue in alternate months. The scene ends with a discussion between the elder daughters which reveals them as determined to take in hand the erratic behaviour of Lear's old age.

Commentary

The relationship between parents and children is established as the play's central theme, linking a number of issues: legitimacy, natural order, love, self-knowledge, justice and authority. The mutable character of the king is introduced: cloaked in a style of regal authority he sulks, raves and threatens, while the end of the scene shows Regan and Goneril decisively in charge. And Cordelia's significance is made clear, associated with a notion that runs through the play: the inadequacy of language to represent truth.

had more affected Had more affection for.
Albany This was the northern part of Britain from Yorkshire to Caithness. Cornwall covered the south and south-west. Cordelia was presumably destined to inherit the middle of the country.
equalities . . . moiety The division has been so carefully done that the most careful examination of the two shares wouldn't persuade either of the dukes to covet the other's inheritance.
breeding Parentage.
at my charge My responsibility.

blush'd . . . i.e. because Edmund is illegitimate.

braz'd Hardened.

conceive Understand. Gloucester makes a pun on this in the next line, when he refers to Edmund's mother conceiving a child by Gloucester.

fault Something wrong.

proper Well-made, handsome.

by order of law Legitimate.

some year elder About a year older.

in my account So far as I am concerned.

saucily Presumptuously. Gloucester means to say that although Edmund's birth was not intended, he is nevertheless fond of the child.

good sport at his making He was conceived in sexual pleasure. Edmund himself refers to the notion that sexual passion creates stronger, handsomer children than does the habitual and perhaps automatic intercourse of married life. (See I, 2, 11–14).

study deserving Try to merit your attention. In view of Edmund's subsequent behaviour this is ironic.

out Abroad.

Sennet A kind of fanfare heralding approach or departure. Here it points the fact that Lear is still king.

Attend Bring here.

our darker purpose Our more secret design. 'Our' is used in the sense of the royal 'we'. Lear refers to his intention to give the most to the daughter who shows she loves him most. So far only his decision to divide the kingdom is known. However, the word 'darker' also carries overtones of seriousness.

fast intent Fixed intention.

younger strengths Those both younger and stronger. The dialogue – or lack of it – between strong youth and weak age is a theme of the play.

son . . . Cornwall and Albany are both sons-in-law of Lear but also his 'sons' as peers in relation to the king. Albany turns out to be a truer son than Cornwall.

constant will Firm intention. Lear again emphasizes his determination, perhaps unconsciously hinting thereby at his incipient instability.

several dowers Separate dowries.

amorous sojourn An example of transferred epithet: their stay is not amorous, but amorousness is its cause.

Interest Possession.

Where . . . challenge A difficult line, which seems to mean 'to the one in whom natural feelings (of love for her father)'.

word . . . matter I can say in words.

eye-sight . . . liberty This curious phrase, besides anticipating the theme of blindness and insight so important to the play, also couples that theme with the parallel notions of restriction and freedom. This coupling is made explicit in the character of Edmund, who can well 'see' his own best advantage, which lies in the 'freedom' to do whatever he likes, regardless of the consequences for others, but who is blind to moral values until death opens his eyes.

No less than life As much as life itself. Goneril indulges in a chain of hyperboles.

speech unable i.e., unable to express itself. Ironically Goneril makes the same claim as Cordelia – that her love cannot be expressed – but her hyperboles, compared with Cordelia's plain speech, show her to be false.

all . . . much Everything of the kind I have mentioned.

Love, and be silent This coupling is central to Cordelia's role in the play. Her words and her appearances are minimal but her significance is major.

these bounds Lear points to places on his map.

champains Open plains.

rich'd Enriched. The verb applies to this line and the one following.

wide-skirted meads Broad meadows.

What says our second daughter If Lear is going to distribute territory according to the degree of love exhibited by his daughters it is illogical of him not to wait until he has heard all three. But of course fair distribution is neither his point nor Shakespeare's. The scene's purposes are to show up the different characters of the three women, and to establish Lear's partial and irrational attitudes. His immediate gift to Goneril shows he has already decided on how to split his kingdom but that he enjoys this theatrical exhibition of his power and the renunciation of it.

that self metal The same substance.

names . . . love Describes my love exactly as it is.

comes too short Doesn't make enough of it. Regan also hints here that she has more love than Goneril.

the most . . . sense The most sensitive part of me. A square is a carpenter's exact measure.

More ponderous Heavier. Cordelia means that her love has greater weight than any words could have.

our joy Notice how Lear is quite unashamed about the fact that Cordelia is his favourite daughter – which helps to explain, in part, the violence of his reaction against her.

vines . . . Burgundy Vineyards of France and dairy-herds of Burgundy. Lear describes Cordelia's suitors in terms of their territories. This is in line with his equation between love and territorial reward.

heave . . . mouth Express my true feelings in words. The notion that the verbal expression of love is either impossible or somehow diminishing is intriguing in the work of a playwright of such rhetorical brilliance, and highlights one of Shakespeare's dramatic problems: the interesting presentation of virtue.

Mend your speech Be more explicit.

duties The duties are both Lear's and Cordelia's – his to beget, breed and love, hers to obey, love and honour.

plight Pledge.

I shall never marry In this speech Cordelia expresses a doctrine of fitness and order which reverberates through the play in contrast to the disorder established by Lear's initial misjudgments: giving authority to his daughters, dividing the kingdom according to a false principle. This disorder is continued in the deeds of Goneril and Regan, whose exaggerated speech at once associates them with it.

true Compare Cordelia's use of the word with Regan's (line 69): Cordelia's words are minimal, Regan's extravagant.

Hecate A goddess in Greek mythology with extensive powers, she came to be associated mainly with witchcraft and the underworld.

operation Influence.

From By virtue of.

Propinquity Near relationship.

The barbarous . . . appetite Scythian is a general term for barbarian. The reference is to parents eating their children, an ironic reversal of what is to happen – metaphorically – to Lear.

generation Offspring.

messes Food.

sometime Former.

Dragon The dragon is a symbol of ferocity – but this may be a reference to Lear's coat of arms.

set my rest Throw myself.

nursery Care.

Hence . . . Who stirs? Lear here shows clear signs of his temperamental nature. Everyone is stunned by his violence.

digest Include.

marry her Provide her with a husband. The deep contradictions in Lear's mind are apparent here. He constantly refers to his daughters in terms of property, while making strenuous emotional demands on all around: he wants to be loved for himself while encouraging such love with material rewards.

large effects . . . troop with Magnificent extras that are connected with.

by monthly course In alternate months.

With reservation of Reserving.

th'addition to Titles and ceremonies of.

sway Power.

Lov'd as my father . . . Kent here reminds us that a king is the father of his people, not only of his own children. This hints at a further dereliction of duty. According to the divine right theory, a king is appointed by God: he cannot, therefore, simply divest himself of office when he feels like it.

make from Move away from.

fork Arrow-head.

unmannerly Rude. The alliteration with 'mad' emphasizes the blunt honesty of Kent – an alliteration taken up at the end of line 145: unmannerly, mad, man.

plainness Plain-speaking. Notice how Goneril, Regan, Cordelia and Kent all make a point of 'plain-speaking' – and with what different effects.

duty . . . folly Despite his plain speaking Kent uses sophisticated language and balanced lines. He generalizes Lear's situation in a sequence of abstract nouns – duty, dread, power, flattery, plainness, honour, majesty, folly. This adds dignity to his words. raising them above a merely personal complaint.

Reserve thy state Keep your regal power. Kent foresees problems if Lear abdicates.

best consideration Careful thought

answer . . . judgment I'll stake my life on this view.

Reverb no hollowness Do not resonate from emptiness. This is Kent's variation on the saying 'Empty vessels make the most noise' i.e. Goneril and Regan.

pawn Stake.

Out of my sight! The second allusion in the play to eyesight – immediately taken up by Kent.

blank The white spot in the middle of an archery target. Kent may be taking up Lear's allusion to archery (l. 142). The implication here is that Lear's eye is wandering from the proper object of its attention.

Apollo The Greek sun-god, patron of medicine, music, poetry and – interestingly – archery. This is one of many references to the gods of Olympus which establish the play's pagan setting.

vent clamour Make noises. Kent shows no sign of softening his tone in response to Lear's rage.

recreant Apostate.

durst Ventured.

strain'd Strained to the limit.

Which . . . bear Which neither our nature nor our royal dignity can put up with.

Our . . . good Our royal authority being maintained. This is a good example of Lear's inability, in practice, to surrender the power he has just bestowed on his daughters and sons-in-law.

disasters Hardships.

trunk Body.

Jupiter The king of the Roman gods. Shakespeare indifferently mixes Greek and Roman names to get his pagan effect.

Fare . . . new Kent goes into rhyming couplets, a common technique in Shakespeare for a character taking elegaic leave.

large Exaggerated.

approve Prove true.

shape . . . new Do there as he has here i.e. speak his mind.

Flourish A kind of fanfare.

dear There is a pun here on personal and financial value.

her price is fallen In this speech Lear makes explicit his equation between love and power, expressed in terms of the property women took to their husbands on marriage as a dowry.

little-seeming substance This seems to be a pun. On the one hand Lear refers to Cordelia's slightness of stature and on the other hand he sarcastically describes her as one who pretends to sincerity by refusing to speak. 'Little-seeming' means 'lacking in display' – 'substance' merely to the 'human form'.

piec'd Into the bargain.

may fitly like May be suitable to.

She's there Lear strikes an offended, contemptuous note here.

owes Admits to. Cordelia's 'infirmities' presumably include the lack of love Lear expects and the poverty to which he has just reduced her.

Election . . . conditions No one can choose under such circumstances. Burgundy's retreat is strongly contrasted with France's generosity.

For you In your case.

make . . . stray Wander so far.

T'avert . . . way To direct your love to someone worthier.

Nature i.e. Cordelia's behaviour is so unnatural.

best object The one you loved most. More temperate than Kent, France puts the sensible view.

argument Topic.

dismantle . . . favour Tear off so many layers of goodwill.

monsters it Makes a monster of it. France picks up his own word 'monstrous' from line 216. He stresses the unnaturalness of Lear's behaviour in this speech.

your fore-vouch'd affection The affection you declared earlier. France is saying that to produce such a reaction Cordelia must have done something really terrible, or the affection Lear earlier described cannot have been real – one or the other. This is a rebuke to the king.

Fall into a taint Must be brought into discredit.

which . . . me. I could never believe that she could do anything wicked, unless a miracle convinced my reason.

for which For lack of which.

lost Spoilt. Paradoxically this intricate speech shows that Cordelia is perfectly capable of speaking her mind. This reminds us that it is specifically a public and *exaggerated* declaration of her love for him she refuses Lear, on the grounds that both exaggeration and publicity would falsify the emotion even as it was expressed.

pleased me . . . Notice Lear's emphasis on the pronoun. He is thinking of himself, not of Cordelia.

tardiness in nature Natural shyness.

history Explanation. Again the scene dwells on the distinction between what is done and what is said. Shakespeare's problem is to show what is not spoken, a major purpose of this scene.

Love's . . . point These words, spoken by a minor character, are vital to an understanding, not only of this play, but of all Shakespeare's later work. Love, says France, is only its true self when it is not mixed with other considerations, such as gain, hatred or passion. Cordelia's subsequent behaviour demonstrates this to be the case. France shows his belief in the doctrine by accepting Lear's daughter without the customary dowry.

regards Respects.

entire Vital.

I am firm This is Lear's problem: he is firm where he should be flexible. It is partly this which leads to the conflict within him.

respect and fortunes Material interests.

Fairest . . . find Like Kent, France goes into rhyming couplets in this speech, from line 253. He also indulges in a number of formal rhetorical devices, notably contrast and paradox: Cordelia is rich because she is poor, choice because forsaken, loved because despised etc.

wat'rish Both productive of streams and also weak. A pun.

unpriz'd precious i.e. Cordelia is unvalued by others but highly valued by France.

although unkind Although they have behaved unnaturally.

where Place.

benison Blessing.

wash'd Tear-wash'd.

professed bosoms Feelings as stated (rather than what I know to be the case).

within his grace In his good affections.

a better place i.e. her own care.

scanted Withheld.

the want Lack of fortune.

And well . . . wanted In other words: you got what you asked for. This haughty sneering sets the tone for Goneril and Regan.

plighted Folded i.e. concealing.

Well . . . prosper! Cordelia's irony is complex. On the one hand she naturally does not wish to see their villainy do well; on the other, it will be better for her father, being in their power, if they are not frustrated.

changes . . . is This can either mean 'Old age has changed him' or 'Old age has made him changeable'.

grossly Evidently.

slenderly Slightly. The two sisters accurately assess their father's weaknesses. Only in the pride and passion of authority do they lose their calculating skill.

of his time Parts of his life i.e. youth and middle age.

long-engraffed condition Firmly rooted state.

therewithal With that.

unconstant starts Fits and starts.

compliment Ceremony.

hit Agree.

carry authority Holds to his power.

with such . . . bears In this temperamental way.

last surrender Recent tantrum. Goneril is already showing her masterful disposition.

i'the heat As soon as possible.

Act I Scene 2

The scene opens with one of the play's most important speeches, in which Edmund invokes the support of the goddess Nature in his ruthless career. Gloucester enters, still mumbling with surprise at Lear's arbitrary violence, and Edmund persuades him of Edgar's treachery by producing a forged letter in which Edgar seems to desire his father's death. The credulous Gloucester is taken in, and so is Edgar, who enters after his father's departure, and is convinced by Edmund that Gloucester is annoyed with him.

Commentary

This takes place the day after Scene 1. Lear has already left the court – his authority has begun to crumble, and the social order with it. Scene 2 introduces the sub-plot and makes the parallels with the plot clear: both Lear and Gloucester turn to their bad children when they feel betrayed by the good ones. But a crucial difference is also made clear: Cordelia falls foul of Lear by her own free will, whereas Edgar is deliberately ensnared by Edmund. This distinction is important: it indicates the higher level on which Lear and Cordelia operate, as free agents who, to some degree at least, choose their fate. Edgar and his father are trapped by a villain, who reveals himself in the scene's opening lines. For Edmund Nature is simply the totality of unrestrained urges and desires backed by strength and luck. In his view there is no difference between men and beasts.

Thou, Nature The notion of nature Edmund expresses here can be summed up in the phrase: might is right.
Stand . . . custom Put up with the nuisance of what is habitual.
curiosity Excessive carefulness.
deprive me i.e. of my inheritance.
moonshines Months.
Lag of Younger than.
base Being illegitimate, Edmund is technically not an aristocrat. But he also implies here that his bastardy makes him, unfairly, socially inferior.
dimensions Bodily frame.
compact Knit together.
generous The word has associations both of 'nobly-born' and 'bountiful'.
true Well-proportioned.
they This 'they' hints at the 'chip on the shoulder' Edmund suffers

from: he sees himself in competition not only with Edgar but with the world.

lusty . . . nature Lust, which has its way in spite of reason or law, is an attribute of that goddess Nature Edmund invoked in line 1.

More composition Better constitution.

fierce quality Haughty manner.

fops Fools.

'tween . . . wake? The implication is that most children are automatically conceived, when their parents are half-awake. Love children, conceived in the full flood of passion, are superior. This is based on the theory that character and physical being are determined at the moment of conception, hinted at earlier by Gloucester (I,1,23).

is . . . As . . . Is as much to Edmund as to Edgar.

speed Go well.

gods A general invocation of all the pagan deities who were, of course, multi-purpose; unlike the God of Christianity who supports only the virtuous.

stand . . . bastards! Edmund somewhat resembles Iago in *Othello*, especially in the fierce, theatrical, even darkly humorous quality of his speeches. He is indeed as vigorous an animal as he says he is. This soliloquy is sardonic and self-consciously wicked.

choler Anger.

prescrib'd Restricted.

exhibition A limited amount. Kent and Gloucester both make the point, echoed by the fool, that there's something wrong in an absolute monarch submitting himself to restriction.

gad Spur of the moment.

put up Put away. This is naturally calculated to arouse Gloucester's curiosity.

terrible despatch Tremendous speed.

nothing A curious echo of Lear (I, 1, 86).

all o'erread Completely read.

to blame Blameworthy.

essay or taste Trial or test.

policy and reverence of Policy of venerating.

best of our times i.e., youth.

idle and fond Useless and foolish.

suffer'd Allowed (i.e. by younger men).

breed Devise.

character Writing.

fain Rather.

perfect Mature.

Abhorred Atrocious.

Unnatural Edmund has neatly transferred his own 'unnaturalness' to Edgar.

I do not . . . Edmund increases his own stock by appearing to intercede for his brother.

run . . . course Be on surer ground.

shake . . . obedience Destroy the core (or basic vestiges) of his obedience (to you).

pawn Wager.

feel Try out.

meet Suitable.

auricular Through the ear i.e. Gloucester can be sure of the truth by secretly listening.

wind . . . him Get to know what he thinks.

unstate myself . . . resolution Give up my position to be certain.

presently Immediately.

convey Arrange.

as . . means In whatever way I can.

late Recent. Gloucester here develops a theme he pursues throughout the play: the relation between men's actions and the influence of heaven, whether of the gods or the stars.

Nature Gloucester's meaning is not Edmund's (see I, 2, 1). The 'wisdom of Nature' refers to man's knowledge *of* nature, acquired partly by observation and partly by reason. By extension, the phrase can thus mean 'the faculty of reason', given to man by Nature, the creator of all things. In line 102, the word refers to that which has been created i.e. the natural world.

sequent Following. We can explain the eclipses but we are still affected by them.

bond This bond is, of course, a product of Nature, but one which is confirmed by reason as well as natural affection. See also I, 1, 92.

comes under Acts according to.

falls . . . nature Goes against nature. i.e. by abdicating and disowning Cordelia.

machinations, hollowness Plotting, deceitfulness.

offence, honesty This reversal – honesty is now a crime – echoes France's comments on Cordelia (I, 1, 249 and 260). Lear's madness has turned the world upside-down.

foppery Foolishness.

sick in fortune Unfortunate.

surfeits Consequences.

on Through.

spherical predominance The ascendancy of a planet at the time of our birth.

divine thrusting on Supernatural determination. Having invoked the goddess Nature in his first soliloquy (I, 2, 1–22) Edmund here develops his theory. In his view Nature stands for the unfettered free will, as opposed to the heavenly determinism invoked by Gloucester. This is one aspect of the play's dialogue between unbridled self-interest and reverence for destiny.

whoremaster Lecherous.

compounded Had intercourse with.

dragon's tail In fiery lust.

Ursa major A constellation. Notice how Edmund's thoughts revert to his own conception and consequent station. Extramarital lust stands symbolically for the free play of the will. Yet Edmund has already told us that the circumstances of his conception made him a better man than his brother. He is merely substituting one theory for another which looks to us very like it.

Fut! Nonsense.

pat Just on time.

cue Hint. The sequence of theatrical metaphors here – pat, catastrophe, cue – point up Edmund's relish of his own energetic villainy, as he shares the joke with the audience.

Tom o'Bedlam The generic name for madmen.

eclipses The echo of Gloucester shows the contempt in which Edmund holds him. The last part of this scene is imbued with black comedy.

fa . . . mi The names of musical notes. Edmund sings to suggest he doesn't know Edgar is approaching.

this other The other.

succeed Follow.

amities Friendships.

diffidences Suspicions.

dissipation of cohorts Desertion of soldiers.

sectary astronomical Devotee of astrology.

When saw . . . Edmund's abrupt change of subject shows him dominating the situation, creating an atmosphere of disturbance and unease.

forbear Shun. This will, of course, make Gloucester even more suspicious.

qualified Cooled.

with . . . person If he were to see you.

continent forbearance Restrained approach.

fitly At a suitable time. Edmund skilfully presents himself as a good friend to Edgar through the very means he is using to betray him.

to the best For the best.

meaning Purpose.

image and horror of it The dreadful truth of the matter.

practices Plots.

wit Skill.

All . . . fit Everything is good to me if I can adapt it to my ends. Edmund ends the scene with a reassertion of his immoral ruthlessness.

Act I Scene 3

Goneril expresses her annoyance at Lear's behaviour, and tells Oswald, her steward, to neglect the king in order to provoke him and give her an excuse for keeping him in order.

Commentary

The scene leads on from Goneril's conversation with Regan at the end of Scene 1 and shows her heading for a collision with Lear. It also establishes her as the stronger and more positive of the two sisters.

come slack Fall short.
fault Offence.
answer Answer for.
I'd ... question I'd like things to come to a head.
distaste Dislike.
Idle Silly.
That ... away! Goneril puts her finger on part of Lear's problem — power without responsibility — but shows no tact in dealing with it.
checks as Reproof instead of.
seen abus'd Seen to be deluded.
grows Comes.
To hold my very course To do the same as me.

Act I Scene 4

Kent enters, in disguise, and takes service with his old master, supporting him in a quarrel with Goneril's steward Oswald. One of Lear's knights reminds the king that he and his retinue are being treated with contempt, and the Fool supports this by telling Lear that he was wrong to abdicate and must expect the worst. At this point Goneril enters and picks a quarrel with her father about his disorderly knights, reducing the number she will receive from one hundred to fifty, arousing Lear's violent hatred and reducing him to tears. He decides to turn to Regan, but Goneril forestalls him by sending Oswald with a letter to her sister, warning her what to expect. Albany expresses doubts about his wife's treatment of the king, but she is resolute.

Commentary

The appearance of the Fool in this scene coincides with the onset of Lear's torment and the beginning of his voyage of self-discovery. When Goneril shows her true colours, the king begins to perceive his mistake in rejecting Cordelia, and his emotional instability manifests itself with surprising violence in the disproportion between cause (lack of respect) and reaction (hysteria, tears, self-doubt). Lear's self-questioning is extended into his fantastic dialogues with the Fool, and the play's language begins to take on the rich, complex, even surrealist qualities which are so important in Acts III and IV.

as well i.e. as well as being in disguise.

defuse Disguise.

raz'd my likeness Concealed my true appearance.

where i.e. by Lear.

full of labours Ready for hard work.

A man Kent and Lear here open the dialogue which continues through the play, about identity. Change of clothes, at first a plot mechanism, becomes in Lear's speeches a profound symbol for exploring the nature of man.

What ... profess? What is your occupation?

I do ... fish The first speech of the play to depart from its comparative realism. Kent, Edgar, Lear and – above all – the Fool all have such fantastic, playful speeches which express the play's wisdom in riddles, conceits and flights of imagination. Kent, true to his character, is the most pithy and sturdy in expression.

trust A position of trust.

wise ... little A hint at Cordelia's situation.

judgment This may be on earth or in heaven.

choose i.e. choose otherwise.

eat no fish Eat well – fish being considered an inferior diet to meat.

You Kent addresses Lear with the more respectful 'you' – Lear addresses Kent familiarly as 'thou'.

countenance Manner – the whole demeanour, not just the face.

Authority This is Kent's secret reproof of Lear, who should not have given up his crown.

counsel Secret.

mar ... it Spoil a complex story in the telling.

sirrah Patronizing form of 'sir'.

clotpoll Blockhead.

that mongrel i.e. Oswald.

roundest Rudest.

entertain'd Treated.

general dependents Household.

my duty i.e. my duty makes me speak. Transferred epithet.

rememb'rest Remindest.

a most faint This can either mean 'slight' or 'indifferent'.

very pretence Positive intention.

Since ... away A link is here established between Cordelia and the Fool. He speaks in riddles what she implies by her silence. They never appear together.

Who am I? Although the question is here asked in the schoolmasterly manner (Tell me what I just said), this question echoes through the play, its irony turned to tragic perplexity.

My lady's father Oswald's answer shocks Lear with the recognition that he is no longer king. They are no longer thought of as his daughters: instead he appears as their father. The different emphasis is vital.

base . . . player Football was a vulgar street game in the 16th century. Notice the word 'base' echoing Edmund's speech in I, 2, 10.

differences i.e. the difference in rank between Oswald and Lear.

lubber Oaf.

earnest Money in advance.

coxcomb A fool's cap – with a cock's comb on its top.

smile . . . sits Make the best of it.

catch cold You'll fare badly. It is impossible to translate the Fool's words exactly, so complex is the web of slang, catch-phrases and 17th century usage. His constant refrain is clear enough, however: Lear has made a fool of himself by giving power to his daughters and neglecting Cordelia.

banish'd Lear is the one who is banished – from his crown and from the affection of his daughters. The Fool is ironic.

a blessing i.e. by marrying her to France and getting her out of the kingdom.

Nuncle A childish version of 'uncle'.

There's mine i.e. Lear hasn't even kept a coxcomb back. This is a hint of what will happen to his hundred knights.

the whip Fools were unfortunate: they had licence to speak freely, but if they went too far could be whipped.

Truth's a dog . . . stink The Fool distinguishes the dog Truth, and the bitch (Goneril + Regan) who lives in luxury.

A . . . me Lear is thinking of Oswald.

gall Bitterness.

Speak . . . knowest Again a reminiscence of Cordelia.

owest Own.

trowest Believe.

Set Stake.

And . . . score You will get more than twenty shillings to the pound. The burden of this series of rhymed proverbs is caution: a warning to Lear against his wild behaviour – though also part of a fool's stock in trade of jokes, sayings and saws.

unfee'd Unpaid. Lawyers give no opinions if not paid.

motley The parti-coloured dress of a jester.

that . . . with This may mean either that we are all born fools, or that Lear in particular was.

will not let me . . . i.e. because they are fools too.

crowns The Fool plays on various meanings of crown: top of the head, ends of an egg, regal coronet.

clovest Chopped.

like myself Foolishly. Whenever the Fool appears there is ambiguity in the use of the word 'fool': a licensed jester who speaks wisdom in riddles, and an unwise person.

had . . . year Were never less in favour.

wear Use.

apish Either 'idiotic' or 'imitative' i.e. of fools. The Fool returns often to the theme that there is no need for jesters when wise men e.g. Lear, have taken their place.

used it Been like that.

lie The Fool, who tells the truth, says he wants to lie i.e. flatter. This is exactly opposite to Regan and Goneril who proclaim their truthfulness but do lie and flatter. The Fool takes up this point in his next lines.

frontlet Headband i.e. frown.

pretty Fortunate.

O . . . figure Cipher.

nothing The Fool puts the truth in a phrase. Lear is nothing but a man, as Kent said he was (I, 4, 10).

sheal'd peascod Empty pod.

allowance Approval.

if you should If you would i.e. encourage such behaviour.

nor . . . sleep Nor the remedies be neglected.

in . . . weal Because of my tender regard for a sound commonwealth.

their working i.e. the remedies. Goneril is telling Lear that if he doesn't sort out his knights she will take steps against them which will be embarrassing for him.

that . . . proceeding i.e. if I *do* have to act everyone will realize that my actions are inevitable. As the Fool has just foretold, she speaks like a mother rebuking a child.

The . . . young An obvious – and cheeky – reference to Lear and Goneril.

darkling In the dark. A reference, perhaps, to Lear's renunciation of power.

Are you our daughter? This simple question raises a number of issues. The implied tone is a mixture of outrage and irony. Lear obviously doesn't notice that Goneril's selfishness is a reflection of his own wilful behaviour: in that sense she is indeed his daughter. On the other hand, she lacks the capacity he demonstrates later in the play for achieving humility. The question naturally leads us to speculate on the mysterious nature of heredity. How can Lear and Gloucester produce such varied children? Paternity is, indeed, a theme of the play.

a cart . . . horse Things are back to front.

Whoop . . . thee A snatch of nonsense, perhaps from a song.

Does any . . . am? One of the play's most famous speeches, these lines take up the hints offered already and formulate them into Lear's final question. The Fool gives him an answer (Lear's shadow) but the real answer is found in the body of the play: Lear himself must find out who he is.

eyes One of the many references to moral or spiritual blindness.

notion Reasoning power.

discernings Intellectual faculties.

lethargied Dulled.

Which Whom – taking up Lear's 'I'.

admiration Pretended surprise.

savour Manner.

pranks Goneril's language – like the Fool's – constantly implies that Lear is a naughty child who must be disciplined.

debosh'd Debauched.

shame . . . remedy i.e. so outrageous is this behaviour it cries out for remedy.

disquantity Reduce.

depend Be your dependants.

besort Be appropriate to.

know themselves i.e. understand their proper dignity.

Degenerate bastard! Apart from the shocking and sudden violence of Lear's language – which suggests he is indeed a little deranged – the interesting point here is his implication that Goneril is not his 'true' child.

kite A bird of prey.

thou liest! It is not made entirely clear whether Goneril has a good case or not. Nevertheless, one can understand the problems of accommodating one hundred energetic men for a month!

parts Qualities.

exact regard Insignificant detail.

worships Honours.

small fault He is already regretting Cordelia – but for the wrong reason: because he can't have his way with Goneril.

engine An instrument of torture.

frame of nature This phrase appears to mean 'natural disposition'. The words 'fix'd place' in that case would refer to the time and state in which he loved Cordelia.

my people i.e. fetch my people.

I am guiltless Albany is sharply distinguished from Cornwall as an honourable man.

Nature Lear, like Edmund, addresses the goddess. She resembles Edmund's goddess as much and as little as the God of one Christian resembles the God of another i.e. as a general creating and directing power with variable characteristics.

derogate Debased.

teem Bear children.

thwart disnatur'd Wrong-headed, unnatural. Lear is praying that Goneril's child will behave to her as she – he thinks – is behaving to him.

cadent Falling.

fret Wear down.

untented Incurable. A tent is a pad of lint.

eyes . . . out Here we have an anticipation of Gloucester's fate.

temper Moisten.

flay . . . visage Lear doesn't notice the anomaly of meeting Goneril's cruelty with a savage metaphor of his own. There is a sense in which Goneril and Regan are recognizably the daughters of this violent man.

Thou . . . ever It is not clear here whether Lear means that Regan will help him to be king again, or merely that she will allow him his full retinue of knights. In both cases he is wrong.

A fox Lear compared Goneril to a wolf. The image of vermin runs throughout the play.

This man Goneril is being sarcastic.

politic Wise.

At point Fully armed.

dream Delusion.

buzz Rumour.

in mercy At risk.

Let me . . . taken I'd rather reduce the danger than worry about its possible consequences.

compact Strengthen. Goneril gives Oswald the broadest hint to tell whatever lies seem appropriate.

under pardon If you'll allow me to say so.

You are . . . mildness You will be more attacked for your lack of wisdom than praised for dangerous gentleness.

better Improve.

th'event We'll see.

Act I Scene 5

Lear makes his arrangements to leave Goneril for Regan, though the Fool expresses doubt that this will make any difference. The king wonders if Goneril's 'cruelty' is beginning to affect his mind.

Commentary

The Fool's constant banter enriches what would otherwise be a scene of mere business, providing a context for Lear's prayer against madness, and a counterpoint for the conversation the king is having with himself.

kibes Chilblains.

thy wit . . . slip-shod i.e. Lear need not fear his brains chilling because he hasn't got any (*slip-shod* i.e. in slippers).

kindly A pun on the two meanings: lovingly, and according to her nature – which is the same as Goneril's.

crab Crab-apple.

She will taste . . . She will behave . . .

I did her wrong It is uncertain whether Lear refers to Regan or to Cordelia. Since he doesn't check the Fool's rude remarks about Regan, he presumably means Cordelia.

horns Lear, being a father, must have been married. All married men, in the Fool's humorous world, are cuckolds. Horns are the sign of the cuckold.

I will forget my nature Lear means to say that he will be a cruel father, not a kind one, but the remark is also ironic in two senses. As Kent said in I, 1, Lear has already forgotten his nature by renouncing his crown. And he forgets it further during his madness, after which he has to rediscover himself.

asses Servants.

To take't again . . . i.e. his kingdom (see also I, 4, 307). Lear is now feeling the consequences of his actions and discovering that there is more to renouncing the crown than giving up work.

mad A hint of what is to come.

temper Balance.

Revision questions on Act I

1 What difference between the characters of Goneril and Regan do you notice *by the end of the first scene*?

2 Do you think that Cordelia was churlish, or at least unsympathetic, in failing to humour her old father, or do you consider that she was right to be firm for a principle that he would not understand?

3 Comment on the conduct of Goneril and Lear in the breach between them.

4 What, in general, is the point of the Fool's sallies in Scenes 4 and 5? Give examples.

Act II Scene 1

Edmund and Curan discuss the rumours of a war between Albany and Cornwall, and when Curan tells Edmund that Cornwall and Regan will reach Gloucester's house that night, Edmund decides to advance his plot against Edgar, who enters providentially at that moment. Edmund stages a fight which makes Gloucester think that Edgar is a traitor, while causing Edgar to think that he should escape from his father's wrath. The plot works: Edgar's flight convinces Gloucester of his legitimate son's guilt, and the old man agrees to make Edmund his heir. Regan and Cornwall arrive and promise support in Gloucester's attempt to apprehend Edgar. They then turn to discussion of the reason for their visit: reports of dissension between Lear and Goneril.

Commentary

In this scene the plot and the sub-plot come together, though Gloucester is still on the side of Cornwall and Edmund, and the two stories are moving at different speeds. The atmosphere of tension and conflict grows.

ones News. The word is used properly, as a plural.
ear-bussing Whispered.
toward Imminent.
perforce Forcibly.
And I . . . must act There is one thing I must do which requires great care.
Briefness Speed.
Upon his party On his side. Edmund creates an impression in Edgar's mind that danger threatens on all sides.
quit you well Fight as well as you can.
Yield . . . here Spoken loudly for Gloucester's benefit.
Of . . . endeavour That I have been fighting fiercely.
conjuring Invoking. Edmund plays on Gloucester's superstitious nature.
Look, Sir Edmund distracts Gloucester's attention so Edgar may escape; Edgar captured might reveal the truth.
Spoke with Spoke about.
bond See I, 1, 92 and note the ironic contrast with Cordelia's use of the word.
loathly Loathingly.
fell motion Fierce attack.
prepared Unsheathed.
lanch'd Wounded.
alarum'd Aroused i.e. as by the trumpet opening a tournament.
Bold . . . right Made brave by being in the right.
gasted Alarmed.
and found-dispatch When he is found he shall be killed. Edmund has achieved his objective of condemning Edgar unheard.
arch Master.
stake Place of execution.
pight Determined.
unpossessing Edmund's stress on the contrast between Edgar's status as the true heir and his own as a bastard is revealing. In his invented quotation he neatly attributes to Edgar exactly his own methods of misrepresentation.
faith'd Believed.
what I should deny i.e. the letter (see I, 2, 45–56).
turn . . . To Blame on.
practice Plotting.
must . . . world Must think the whole world very stupid.

pregnant . . . spirits Ready and powerful motives.

fast'ned Determined.

Loyal and natural The irony is complex here. We, the audience, know that Edmund is disloyal to Gloucester. We also know he is behaving 'naturally' in the sense that he is true to his own nature – yet by 'natural' Gloucester means, of course, 'as a son should behave'. There is, besides, a further pun on the meaning of natural as 'legitimate'. Edmund has now replaced Edgar in Gloucester's eyes as his true heir.

capable i.e. of inheriting his father's property.

comes too short Is inadequate – an ironic remark when it comes from Regan.

Was he . . . knights Regan joins in creating Edgar's guilt by association.

ill affected Evilly disposed.

expense Expenditure. Again, this is a doubly ironic remark from Regan, who stints her father though he has given her half his kingdom.

bewray Expose.

his practice Edgar's plot.

make . . . please Invoke my authority to do as you please in the matter.

Natures . . . need Once again Edmund is ironically commended for just the qualities he lacks. The irony is doubled when Cornwall is later revealed to be equally vicious.

first Directly.

Truly Ironic: Edmund first acts in concert with the evil Cornwall and Regan, then tries to play off Regan and Goneril, who both desire him, and finally, reveals their plots at the moment of death.

Thus Regan takes over: she is the stronger partner here.

threading i.e. as if threading a needle, with difficulty.

Occasions Affairs.

prize Importance.

from Away from – in order that Lear may not arrive with his hundred knights and embarrass her.

attend dispatch Are waiting to be sent.

Act II Scene 2

Kent meets Oswald in the early morning at Gloucester's castle where both have been instructed to follow Regan for her replies to the letters of Lear and Goneril, their respective master and mistress. Kent contemptuously rails at Oswald as a flashy upstart, trying to provoke him into a fight. Oswald will not draw his sword and Kent beats him. Oswald's shouts bring in Edmund and Cornwall, who punishes Kent by putting him in the stocks for brawling and insolence. Gloucester is alarmed at the insult offered to the king by stocking his messenger, but Cornwall and Regan, like Lear before them, insist on the exercise of their authority over Kent.

It is still too dark for Kent to read a letter he has from Cordelia: weary, he soon falls asleep.

Commentary

In this scene it is Regan's turn to reveal her brutality, and the distinction between Albany and Cornwall is made clear: where Albany expressed his doubts, Cornwall is ahead of his wife in urging brutal treatment. On the other hand, the symbolic links between Cordelia and Kent, the two characters who favour plain speech, are strengthened by the information that they are corresponding, united in hidden loyalty – Cordelia in France, Kent in disguise.

pinfold Cattle-pen.
A knave . . . Kent's outburst against Oswald is more than a catalogue of insults – though it is magnificently that. He characterizes Oswald as false, superficial and trivial: all that is opposite to the sturdy and honest loyalty of Kent's own character.
eater . . . meats i.e. a menial who eats the left-overs.
three-suited Servants were commonly allowed three suits a year. Kent identifies Oswald as essentially servile. Given that the distinctions between true and false nobility are a theme of the play, the relevance of this charge is clear.
hundred-pound A reference to James I's creation of knights for a £100 fee.
action-taking Fighting by law rather than in person i.e. cowardly.
glass-gazing Vain.
super-serviceable Obsequious.
one-trunk-inheriting Having only one trunkful of goods i.e. poor.
a bawd . . . service Over-zealous.
composition Mixture.
addition Titles.
cullionly barber-monger Base fop i.e. one always at the barber's.
Vanity the puppet i.e. Goneril.
carbonado Slash.
neat Dandified.
matter Quarrel.
goodman boy A term of contempt, as one might say 'Your lordship'.
flesh Blood.
difference Argument.
disclaims Renounces herself i.e. you are unnatural.
tailor With this proverb Kent pursues his theme: that Oswald is no better than a tailor's dummy. This is an instance of the clothing imagery later to be so important in Lear's great speeches.

unnecessary The letter Z, being rarely used, was a literal equivalent to the numerical zero.

unbolted Crude.

jakes Lavatory.

wagtail Kent means to evoke the jerky, nervous movements of this bird.

intrince Woven together.

smooth Encourage. Kent may be thinking of his own opposition to Lear's foolishness.

Renege Deny.

halcyon Kingfisher. This refers to the belief that a suspended dead kingfisher would always turn its beak into the wind.

gale and vary Changing gale.

epileptic Though pale, Oswald is now grinning in safety behind his master Cornwall.

Smoile you my Smile you at my. The spelling may indicate Kent speaking in dialect.

Goose . . . Camelot The specific reference here is unclear, but the general meaning very plain: give me half a chance and I'd soon deal with a goose like you.

Sarum Salisbury.

constrains the garb Forces himself to adopt the manner.

Quite . . . nature Quite out of character. Compare Lear I, 5, 31 and elsewhere.

he cannot . . . plain Cornwall speaks sarcastically, as if quoting.

more corrupter Cornwall uses a double superlative for emphasis.

silly-ducking Bowing and scraping.

stretch . . . nicely Do their duty exactly.

Under . . . aspect With your most gracious permission. Kent is mocking the style of florid compliment common in 17th century courts.

Phoebus The Greek sun god, to whom Kent is sarcastically comparing Cornwall, and by whom Lear swore, I, 1, 158.

dialect Natural tongue.

discommend Disapprove.

though I . . . to't An obscure passage, probably meaning: though I should convert you to like me so much that you would ask me to flatter you.

put . . . man Talked himself up as such a brave man.

worthied him Made him appear worthy.

For . . . self-subdu'd For controlling someone who was controlling himself.

fleshment Excitement. Oswald implies that once the braggart Kent tasted blood, he wanted more.

Ajax . . . fool i.e. Ajax (a great Grecian warrior in the Trojan war) is a fool compared with them.

grace and person The royal status and the character.

colour Type. Regan associated Edgar with the rowdy knights. Here

Cornwall does the same for Kent. Lear is gradually being identified as the focus for their resentment.

low Undignified. Kent is, after all, Lear's servant, even though in disguise.

rubb'd Hindered. Gloucester gives us an insight into the violence of Cornwall's character horribly vindicated when the duke puts out Gloucester's own eyes.

saw Saying.

Thou ... sun i.e. Lear comes out of the church's pleasant shade into the unrelenting sun – ironically taking up the earlier reference to Cornwall as Phoebus (II, 2, 104).

obscured Incognito. Kent here fills in both the plot and Cordelia's situation.

enormous Unusual.

and shall ... remedies The sense is obscure: the meaning is that Cordelia will find means of delivering them from their distresses (*losses* i.e. misfortunes).

vantage The opportunity.

Fortune ... wheel! Kent here invokes that image of the wheel of Fortune which is so important to the whole play.

Act II Scene 3

Edgar, proclaimed an outlaw, decides to escape by disguising himself as a mad beggar, Tom o'Bedlam.

Commentary

Edgar proclaims his intention in a soliloquy which also gives the audience necessary information about his change of status and fills in the time between Kent's stocking and Lear's discovery of him.

Kent has already assumed a disguise; now Edgar does so. This is clearly significant in a play so concerned with the nature of true and false identities. Edgar's language anticipates Lear's meditations on poverty, suffering, justice and authority in Act IV.

proclaim'd i.e. as a criminal.

attend my taking Wait to take me prisoner.

am bethought Have it in mind.

in ... man To show how contemptible man is.

elf Involve.

presented Open.

proof Example.

Bedlam The famous madhouse.

object Appearance.
pelting Insignificant.
bans Imprecations.
Enforce Urge or demand.
Turlygod No one has explained this term. It may mean simply 'madman'.
That's . . . yet There's still a chance if I take this disguise.
Edgar . . . am A play on words, meaning both: If I stay as Edgar I'll be killed *and* I'll not be Edgar any more.

Act II Scene 4

Having followed Regan from her home to Gloucester's castle, Lear finds Kent in the stocks outside. He cannot believe Regan and Cornwall have put him there and, almost overcome with emotion, goes in to find out. Regan and Cornwall, however, instruct Gloucester to inform the incredulous Lear that they cannot see him. Incensed by the sight of Kent in the stocks, Lear angrily orders Gloucester to fetch them without fail, and he does so. They greet Lear coldly and Kent is set free.

Lear complains of Goneril to Regan, who tells him to return to her sister. Lear lambasts Goneril and argues with Regan, who refuses to give way. Oswald arrives, shortly followed by Goneril herself, and the two sisters support one another in arguing that not only should Lear reduce his retinue, but that he should even disperse it completely, sparking off his great speech at line 262. The king tries to be patient, but it is not in his nature and he is near breaking point. He leaves as the storm is heard breaking in the distance. Regan and Cornwall instruct Gloucester to close his doors and come inside. The ties between Lear and his two daughters are severed.

Commentary

This scene concludes the working out of the main plot: in the remaining acts we see the consequences of what has so far occurred. Lear now knows the full truth about Regan and Goneril and his mind is on the verge of collapse, unable to cope with the fact that nothing is what it seemed to be. The sound of the storm signals that collapse. Up to now the play has been relatively realistic in manner. This changes in Act III, when the symbolic and poetic aspects come to the surface, dominated by the mad Lear, the Fool, and the feignedly mad Edgar.

cruel A pun on cruel and crewel – a worsted material used for garters.
over-lusty Too lively.
nether-stocks Stockings.
Jupiter . . . Juno King and queen of the Roman gods.
which way . . . us How you could deserve such treatment, as our
  messenger, or how they could impose it.
commend Deliver.
reeking post Sweating messenger.
Stew'd Sweltering.
spite of intermission In spite of interrupting my business.
presently At once.
on whose As a result of the.
meiny Household.
Display'd . . . against Behaved . . . to.
man than wit Manhood than sense.
Winter's . . . way There's still trouble ahead if that's the way things are
  going.
Father . . . kind Fathers who bestow their property on their children
  will be ignored by those children; fathers who hold fast to what they
  own will keep their children's loyalty.
bear bags Possess money-bags.
dolours A pun on dollars and pains.
mother . . . *Hysterica passio* Both terms for hysteria – thought to
  originate especially in the womb (Greek- *hystera*).
element Rightful place. Here we see the beginning of the madness
  Lear suspected at I, 5, 43.
ant Continuing the winter metaphor from II, 4, 45 the Fool implies
  that Lear, unlike the ant, has not laid up a store of food for the winter
  of his life: therefore his followers desert him.
stinking i.e. in misfortune. Each of the Fool's remarks points to the
  way men ignore or abandon those who have lost their luck.
I would . . . follow it But the Fool doesn't follow his own advice to
  leave those in misfortune, and sticks by Lear.
storm An anticipation of what is to come.
But I . . . perdy In lines important for the whole play, the Fool
  contradicts what he has just said in play: the wise man may run away,
  but the *truly* wise man – who may be called Fool – remains faithful.
knave One who acts contemptibly.
perdy By God.
Not . . . Fool The Fool implies that Kent is as wise as himself.
They . . . night! Lear angrily quotes the excuses.
fetches Pretexts.
images Indications.
quality Temperament.
The King Lear cannot cast off his accustomed authority.
tends This may mean 'intends' i.e. expects.
that – The breaking syntax indicates Lear's passion. This becomes
  acute at the height of his madness.

he is not well Lear looks for excuses: he cannot believe Cornwall guilty of such insolence.

office Duty.

Whereto ... bound Which depends on our good health.

we are ... body These lines, about the relationship between mental and bodily suffering, foreshadow Lear's own agony on the heath.

remotion Removal.

practice Deviousness. Notice how Lear oscillates violently from one view to its opposite: suspicion, forgiveness, then suspicion again.

Till ... death Until the noise makes sleep impossible.

my rising heart See II, 4, 55 above.

cockney Foolish woman.

knapp'd Knocked.

coxcombs Heads.

buttered his hay i.e. in order to prevent the horses eating it, ostlers sometimes greased the hay. But the brother in the Fool's story does it out of 'kindness' – as foolish as Lear.

Good morrow Lear's words are ironic: it is now evening.

Sepulchring Being the sepulchre. One of the play's many references to parentage and illegitimacy. Lear means that he would not believe Regan to be his child, were she ungrateful. This is ironic, in view of the wilfullness she has very evidently inherited from her father.

naught i.e. both 'worthless' and 'of no account to me'.

vulture This refers to the Greek myth in which Prometheus was punished by Zeus with a vulture who gnawed his liver.

You less ... duty You undervalue her more than she neglects her duty.

fail her Fail in her.

Nature i.e. the force of life.

state Either 'mental condition' or 'obligation'. Regan reverses the roles of parent and child.

forgiveness The tone here is surprised, bitter and ironic. Lear can see nothing to ask forgiveness for.

Age is unnecessary Old people are superfluous. This is a specific instance of the general doctrine Lear enunciates in his speech at II, 4, 263–84. Ironic.

unsightly Even Regan is embarrassed by her father's kneeling.

abated Deprived.

ingrateful top Ungrateful head.

young bones This phrase may either refer to Goneril herself or to her unborn children (see I, 4, 276).

Taking Infectious. Note that there is some justice in Regan's charge of irresponsibility: Lear's tone is not only bitter but also fretful, and his language extreme.

fen-suck'd Sucked up from the fens.

tender-hefted Gentle-bodied.

scant my sizes Reduce my share.

oppose the bolt Shut the door.

offices Obligations.

Effects Manifestations.

whose . . . follows i.e. Oswald takes Goneril as his model in the matter of insolent pride.

Who comes here? Lear has apparently not noticed Regan's comment at l.181 – he is too preoccupied with Oswald and Kent.

it i.e. old age.

finds Calls.

disorders Misbehaviour.

seem so Behave accordingly i.e. be quiet and docile.

out of Unprovided with.

wolf and owl Predators are common in the play's imagery. Here Lear prefers them to his daughters.

Necessity Lear foreshadows the heart of the play when he, Gloucester and Edgar contend with the elements in different ways.

afoot Going.

sumpter Drudge.

Or . . . flesh Lear here expresses very vividly one of the play's basic assumptions: that ties of blood have absolute demands, and cannot be disowned without serious consequences.

embossed Swollen.

corrupted Diseased. There is also a pun here, because 'blood' can mean descendants. Goneril is therefore, in a moral sense, Lear's corrupted blood.

thunder-bearer . . . Jove Both references to the Roman king of the gods who showed his displeasure by hurling thunderbolts. This, and similar references, anticipate the storm scene.

with Regan His hostility to Goneril has obscured Lear's perception of Regan's equal but more diplomatic opposition.

those i.e. people of common sense.

mingle . . . passion Look at your passion reasonably.

and so – Regan cannot be bothered to complete the argument, realizing that old age is hardly good cause for what she and her sister are doing.

avouch Assert.

sith that As.

Hold amity Get on. Regan changes the ground of her argument to more practical complaints about the expense and rowdiness of the knights.

slack ye Be neglectful of their duty to you.

Stands . . . of Deserves some.

twice her love Lear's pathetic measuring of love in material terms is here shown up for what it is.

What need one? Regan's question is the only logical conclusion, providing the stark starting-point for the speech that follows.

O! reason not . . . This is the first in the series of Lear's great speeches on the road to self-discovery. In the first part he asserts a central notion of what constitutes human life: something more than mere existence. At line 269 he shows signs of breaking under the stress of his emotion. In the second half he utters furious threats against his daughters. Breaks of syntax such as line 278 show him to be on the verge of madness.

superfluous Contrast this with Gloucester's words at IV, 1, 66. Gloucester's superfluity is an excess which interferes with true perception. Lear, on the other hand, is talking about the essential dignity of human life – that which sets it apart from the beasts. But it is just this 'extra' quality which is questioned in the play.

nature . . . warm You would not need the flimsy but grand clothes you have on.

true need Lear breaks off before explaining the difference between the essential and the unnecessary, exemplified in Regan's rich attire. The clothing metaphor is central to the play.

fool . . . much Don't make me such a fool as.

I'll not weep But he has already wept – at I, 4, 295.

a storm The beginning of the storm is synchronized with the onset of the king's madness, which at first vents itself in rage. Note how many premonitions Lear has of his derangement e.g. I, 4, 222; I, 5, 42; II, 4, 55; II, 4, 216; II, 4, 284; III, 2, 67 etc.

the old man Regan's contemptuous reference to her father, all pretence of respect now abandoned.

bestow'd Accommodated.

taste Feel the results of.

For his particular On his own.

Do sorely ruffle Blow very strongly.

themselves procure Bring on themselves.

apt . . . abus'd Easily misled.

Revision questions on Act II

1 In what ways was Kent's service of little value to Lear? Do you think he deserved being put in the stocks?

2 Do you consider Edmund's deception of Gloucester and Edgar in Acts I and II too easy to be credible? Give reasons.

3 Comment on the conduct and manner of Regan and Lear in the breach between them at the end of this act.

Act III Scene 1

Kent meets a gentleman on the heath. The storm is in full progress. The gentleman tells Kent that Lear is with the Fool, exposed to the storm, and Kent asks the Gentleman to go to Dover to meet Cordelia and her husband, France, who have landed secretly with an army, and to tell them about Lear's situation and condition. The gentleman agrees, and he and Kent decide first to find the king.

Commentary

The scene is largely for the purpose of conveying information – including what was no doubt included in Cordelia's letter to Kent, and to show that Lear is not without friends. It also gives a magnificent verbal picture of the storm and of the pathetic state of the king at large in it. The vocabulary of wild beasts is typical of a play in which the nature of man is being tested.

main Mainland.
things Ambiguous: this may refer to 'the situation as it is' or 'things in general'.
make nothing of Ambiguous: it may mean 'turn into nothing' or 'are indifferent to'.
little world of man The gentleman here makes explicit a comparison between the storm in the world and the storm in Lear. This speech has a choric function: a concerned but detached onlooker describes what he sees. Yet the language he uses – eyeless, nothing, world of man etc. – links his words with the play's complex verbal texture.
to-and-fro-conflicting Furiously stormy.
cub-drawn Suckled dry by her cubs. On a normal night such a bear would look for food: so bad is the weather, even she stays at home.
belly-pinched Hungry. Compared to the wolf, the bear and the lion, Lear is shown to be even fiercer in his anger. Earlier (I, 1, 121) the king compared himself to a frightening beast.
unbonneted Hatless – an especially undignified state in a king, however angry. Lear begins to cast away his clothes.
bids . . . all In other words, Lear literally 'throws everything to the winds'.
labours to out-jest Strives to drive out by jesting.
upon . . . note On the strength of what I know about you.
that . . . stars Whose great fortune.
Which are . . . state Who are spies in the service of France.
snuffs and packings Quarrels and plots.
hard rein Cruel treatment.
furnishings Outward signs. Whether Shakespeare meant the speech to break is not clear; it is certainly obscure. Kent, having mentioned the rift between Albany and Cornwall, the reasons for which are not clear, is explaining the presence of a French army in Britain. Why the break between Albany and Cornwall should bring the French over isn't made clear. The dramatic reason is simply that Shakespeare needs to bring Cordelia back to her father.
scatter'd Divided, both physically and – Kent tells us – politically.

Wise in our negligence Taking advantage of our unpreparedness.
have secret feet Have landed secretly.
at point In readiness.
To show . . . banner To reveal themselves.
If . . . so far If you credit what I say enough.
bemadding Maddening.
plain Complain. The 'sorrow' Lear has to complain of is, of course, the cruel treatment of his daughters.
assurance Reliable information.
Out-wall Appearance.
in which . . . this In which effort, you go that way, and I'll go this way.

Act III Scene 2

On another part of the heath Kent finds Lear defying the elements, accompanied only by the Fool, whose running commentary on Lear's folly continues.

Commentary

Lear identifies the elements with his cruel daughters and feels his wits beginning 'to turn'. Kent persuades his master to enter a hovel for shelter, and the scene ends with a curious prophecy from the Fool in rhyming couplets.

cocks Weather-cocks.
thought-executing Ambiguous: either 'swift as thought' or 'doing the will of your creator'.
Vaunt-couriers Forerunners.
oak-cleaving Note the high proportion of compound epithets in this speech, which give it a torrential, explosive rhetoric of its own.
thunder One of many references in the play. Thunder signifies both the displeasure and the power of the gods.
Nature's moulds i.e. the moulds in which Nature casts the forms of men.
germens Seeds. The speech joins the creation of life and its destruction.
court holy-water Fair words or flattery. Proverbial.
in Let us go in.
thy Lear addresses the storm as a power personified, another manifestation of nature.
tax Charge. Earlier the gentleman linked the world's storm with Lear's state. Here the king extends that comparison negatively.
subscription Obedience.
your slave . . . But yet Lear is confused. The elements owe him nothing, yet they seem to conspire with his two daughters to torment him.

high-engender'd Heaven-born.

The cod-piece ... A literal translation of the song is: 'The man who takes a mistress before he has a house will end with a lousy wife. The man who prefers his toe to his heart will suffer the more from that misjudgment.' The general application of this apparent nonsense is clear: Lear has foolishly chosen Goneril and Regan in preference to Cordelia, ending with the lousy wife and the corn.

cod-piece The part of men's clothing covering the genitals – here signifying the man himself.

house Copulate.

For ... glass Apparently irrelevant, perhaps indicating that men will always be so foolish, just as pretty women will always study themselves in the mirror.

No ... Lear is clearly too preoccupied to notice the Fool.

grace i.e. the king.

Gallow Frighten.

wanderers ... dark Wild animals.

caves See note on III, 1, 12.

Since I was man Kent's speech stresses the unique ferocity of the storm, boding special events.

man's ... fear The immediate meaning is that human nature cannot bear the fear. The more general hint is that this storm disturbs the very nature of man, or at least reflects such disturbance.

pudder Commotion.

perjur'd Perjurer.

simular Counterfeiter.

caitiff Villain.

practis'd on Plotted against.

pent-up Concealed.

Rive Burst open.

continents i.e. that which conceals you.

cry ... grace Beg for mercy from these terrifying officers of vengeance.

summoners Officers who brought people before ecclesiastical courts.

I ... sinning Lear directs the elements to seek out others. He is a victim, he says, not an offender. At this stage of the play he has acquired little self-knowledge.

bare-headed One of many references in the storm scenes to Lear's lack of cover, emphasizing his vulnerability.

Which The inhabitants of which.

demanding When I asked.

scanted Withheld.

My wits ... See note on II, 4, 284.

The ... precious Necessity has the power to make vile things precious. It is necessity Lear is beginning to learn about.

He that has ... This appears to be an adaptation of the song in *Twelfth Night*, V, 1, 398. For once, the meaning is clear.

brave Fine.

I'll speak . . . While these lines contain jokes, riddles and allusions in the Fool's style, they are hardly in the condensed, cryptic manner of his songs, and may be an interpolation by an actor. It is not in the Quarto texts. The speech is muddling: 81–84 describe things as they are, 85–90 refer to a desirable future.

Act III Scene 3

Gloucester, beginning to rebel against Cornwall's treatment of Lear, and worried by the reported strife between Cornwall and Albany, confides to Edmund that he is going to help the king in secret. He also tells him that he has received a letter which, like Kent's from Cordelia, informs him that an army has landed in Britain which will revenge Lear's injuries. Edmund decides to betray his father and turn this confidence to his own advantage.

Commentary

There is a symmetry between Gloucester and Edmund, one secretly allying himself with the king and the other with Cornwall.

unnatural Gloucester recognizes Cornwall's behaviour for what it is.
mine own house It appears the behaviour of Cornwall and Regan is as arbitrary as – we are told – Lear's has been.
unnatural There is double irony in Edmund's echo of Gloucester, for we know that he is betraying his father as Regan betrays hers. Besides, he has his own view of what is 'natural' (see I, 2, 22).
division Kent's words (III, 1,19) are confirmed.
a letter Note how much of Edmund's career depends on dangerous letters. He disposes of Edgar with one, traps Gloucester with another, has his plot revealed to Edgar by a third.
home In full.
footed Landed.
privily Secretly.
toward Imminent.
be careful The dramatic irony of these words is revealed in the next speech: Edmund will be careful of his own interests.
This courtesy i.e. Gloucester's help for Lear.
draw Gain.

Act III Scene 4

Again on the heath, Lear, accompanied by Kent and the Fool, meets Edgar disguised as Tom o'Bedlam. Their crazy conversation reveals that Lear is now quite mad, and the king tears off his clothes. Gloucester arrives to find the nearly naked Lear and leads him to shelter, accompanied by Edgar, Kent and the Fool.

Commentary

The conflict between appearance and reality is crucial in this scene. Kent is in disguise; Edgar is also in disguise and pretending to be mad; Lear *is* mad; and the Fool is never a character in the play but a voice, playing with ideas. Only Gloucester is what he seems – and he does not know that he is about to be betrayed for acting in secret against the instructions of Regan and Cornwall. The normal world is turned upside down, reflecting the disorder in Lear himself.

nature Human nature.

free Easy.

delicate Vulnerable. The burden of Lear's sense is that physical effort and pain help to dull mental suffering.

else Other.

mouth ... hand The notion of members of a family being part of the same blood and body is pervasive: for one to turn against another is unnatural, self-destructive.

home In full. It doesn't occur to Lear yet that his desire for vengeance is just as brutal as their ill-treatment.

all,–O! Notice the way in which Lear increasingly seems unable to sustain one line of thought: instead he veers between grief, anger and pride, amazement and incomprehension.

houseless The theme of 'houselessness' recurs often, reinforcing the notion of man's 'unnatural' exposure to nature – an unnatural state of affairs which is, paradoxically, required to bring Lear to some sense, however dim, of what *is* natural i.e. proper to humankind. In this sense a roof – housing – is symbolic of human love and charity.

loop'd and window'd Full of holes.

Too little care ... In the midst of his own grief Lear is brought face to face with his social conscience. It is extraordinary that in this most poetic, even symbolic of Shakespeare's tragedies, such a 'realistic' theme should surface and be developed through Acts III and IV. Personal and social justice are shown to be linked.

this i.e. the state of the poor.

superflux Superfluity.

Fathom and half The huge amounts of rain suggest to Edgar the 'mad' theme of being at sea taking soundings.

Away! From now on Edgar, alias Poor Tom, adds his nonsense to the Fool's, constituting a formidably complex verbal texture at moments of the play, especially in this scene.

Didst thou give all . . . It seems that Lear is now mad, unable to shake off his obsession.

ratsbane Rat poison. Edgar introduces the theme of suicide, on which Gloucester later meditates and which Goneril performs. But he makes it clear here that suicide is a temptation of the devil.

porridge Stew.

course Chase.

five wits Common wit, imagination, fantasy, estimation and memory – matching the five senses.

taking Infection.

There 'Tom' pretends he can see the devil who persecutes him.

reserv'd Kept back. See II, 4, 250.

pendulous Hanging overhead.

thus little . . . flesh Lear surveys Edgar's wretched, semi-naked state.

pelican The pelican is fabulously supposed to feed its young with its own blood. Pelican daughters are therefore especially greedy and fierce, even cannibalistic.

Pillicock . . . loo! Nonsense rhyme.

This cold . . . madmen In contrast to Edgar's nonsense the Fool steps out of his role to speak directly. Thus they both reverse roles, as Lear does in his madness.

commit not i.e. adultery. Edgar recites a litany of the crimes Lear raves about: filial disobedience, lechery, vanity, injustice.

A servingman One may compare this speech of Edgar's with Kent's abuse of Oswald (II, 2, 13–81).

act of darkness Copulation.

out-paramour'd Had more lovers than.

Turk The Sultan – who had a harem of many wives.

light of ear Credulous.

hog . . . Note once again the list of beasts and predators.

creaking . . . silks Creaking shoes and silk dresses were fashionable finery.

plackets Petticoats.

Dolphin A form of Dauphin. The meaning of these lines is obscure.

answer Face.

extremity Intense severity.

Is man . . . Lear's questions continue the debate about the nature of man which figures so largely in the middle of the play. His constant references to animals suggest both comparisons and questions.

silk . . . hide . . . wool These lines anticipate Lear's passionate outburst about clothes and justice (IV, 6, 155–170).

unaccommodated Uncovered. The word also has the wider sense of uncivilized.

forked Two-legged.

naughty Foul.

Flibbertigibbet A devil.

first cock Midnight.

the web and the pin Cataract.

squinies Makes squint.
white Ripening.
Swithhold ... A nonsense rhyme or charm.
aroint thee Away with thee.
sallets Salads.
whipp'd Beggars were liable to be whipped from parish to parish. A tithing was a district with ten families in – roughly a parish.
Smulkin A devil.
Modo ... Mahu Familiar names for Satan – the prince of darkness.
What ... thunder? A very natural question in a storm.
Theban Wise man.
His daughters ... death In the light of his own experience it seems natural to Gloucester that filial cruelty produces madness.
good Kent Kent is present, of course – in disguise. So is Gloucester's son (see line 163 below). This heightens the pathos of Gloucester's remarks.
Athenian A wise man.
Child The son of a knight.
Fie ... Edgar seems to be muddling together an old ballad with words from *Jack the Giant Killer*.

Act III Scene 5

Edmund has met Cornwall in Gloucester's castle and revealed to him his father's 'treachery'. Cornwall vows revenge and promises Edmund the earldom of Gloucester.

Commentary

The depths of Edmund's cynicism and Cornwall's petty vindictiveness are made clear: Shakespeare gives us two carefully distinguished examples of ruthless self-interest. Edmund's dishonesty is compounded by hypocritical arguments about duty and filial obligation; and his reference to treachery shows how he turns all ordinary moral values – as embodied by Kent and Gloucester – on their head.

nature Filial feelings – as opposed to loyalty to Cornwall.
provoking merit A puzzling phrase, it probably means 'something in Gloucester which deserved punishment'.
approves Proves.
intelligent party Informer.
to the advantages of In the service of.
stuff ... fully More completely confirm Cornwall's suspicion.
loyalty ... blood Edmund again mentions the conflict of his loyalties, taking up the theme of natural affection and obligation versus self-interest – which he presents as duty.

Act III Scene 6

In the farmhouse adjoining the castle, where Gloucester has taken the mad king, Lear imagines himself trying Regan and Goneril in the presence of Edgar and the Fool, with Kent, the only one who tries to restrain his master, counselling peace.

Gloucester comes in to say that he has learnt of a plot against the king's life. He begs Kent to take Lear to Dover, where they can meet Cordelia's army. The scene ends with a soliloquy in which Edgar reflects on the nature of suffering in the manner of a chorus.

Commentary

The theme of justice, running through the play, is here made explicit in the crazy trial scene, anticipating Lear's great speeches in Act IV.

piece out Augment. Gloucester will make Lear as comfortable as he can.

Frateretto Another fiend. The nonsense mixed in with Edgar's wisdom is not important in itself, but as fantastic colour.

A King This shows Lear as well aware of his condition. His dementia comes and goes, like a fever, and as such passes when he sleeps.

yeoman Gentleman farmer. The Fool refers to the displacement of the father by the son.

a thousand i.e. devils.

hizzing Hissing.

sapient Wise.

eyes Spectators.

Come . . . to me Edgar sings the first line of a popular song. The Fool breaks in with his own words.

Hoppedance A fiend.

cries His hungry stomach rumbles. Like Lear, Edgar is discovering for the first time what privation is.

take thy place Here we have a kind of play within a play: Edgar, Lear and the Fool act out their parody of a court-room in a way which reflects on the arbitrary injustice of Cornwall and Regan.

yoke-fellow Partner.

o'th'commission Commissioned as a judge.

Sleepest . . . harm Lines from an old song – they seem to have no thematic significance.

I . . . joint-stool A proverbial expression – an apology for overlooking someone.

store Material.

Tray . . . Sweetheart Perhaps the names of the king's dogs.

brach or lym Bitch or bloodhound.

trundle-tail Drooping-tail.

horn is dry Cup is empty i.e. he is too overcome to go on playing the part of Tom o'Bedlam.

entertain Engage.

Persian i.e. foreign, strange.

curtains Lear thinks he is at home.

And ... noon These are the Fool's last words in the play. He leaves 16 lines later.

sinews Nerves. Kent anticipates Lear's sleep in IV, 7.

Stand ... cure Will be hard to cure.

When we ... lurk Edgar here acts both his own role and that of a chorus, meditating on the central tragic theme: the fall of great ones. The speech also brings out the parallels between the Lear and Gloucester plots. Shakespeare often uses a rhyming couplet to end a scene; here, a whole series marks the formal character of the speech.

free Carefree.

sufferance Suffering. Edgar offers his own version of Lear's theory that bodily suffering palliates mental pain. For Edgar, fellows in misery are a help – especially when they are the great. His later meeting with Gloucester makes a mockery of this.

He ... father'd Just as he suffered from cruel children, so I do from a cruel father.

high noises Discordant noises in high places.

thyself bewray Show your true self.

false opinion i.e. Gloucester's suspicion.

thy just proof Proof of your honesty.

repeals Recalls – by repealing sentence of banishment.

reconciles i.e. to his father.

Lurk, lurk A curiously self-conscious injunction – but a good way of breaking the monotony of the couplets at the scene's end, and reintroducing the sinister, poetic note. It takes up the theatricality consistently associated with Edgar.

Act III Scene 7

Cornwall bids Goneril go to her husband with advice to make rapid preparation against the landing of the French army; and sends his servants to find Gloucester. Regan and Goneril cry out for savage revenge against the earl. Oswald seals Gloucester's fate by telling Cornwall that the earl has aided Lear's escape. Cornwall tells Oswald to bind Gloucester and fetch him hither.

Gloucester enters protesting, but he is forced into a seat and questioned by Regan and Cornwall, who puts out one of his eyes. The duke fights an outraged servant who challenges him, but the servant is killed by Regan, and Cornwall puts out Gloucester's other eye, telling the servants to push him out of the house. However, Cornwall has been badly injured in his fight, and is led off, bleeding, by Regan. Two further servants, horrified by the incident, vow to help Gloucester.

Commentary

The apparently gratuitous violence of this scene is central to the play. It underlines the symbolism of blindness and sight, so important to the imagery, and ironically, Gloucester learns the truth about Edmund and Edgar immediately after his blinding. It also shockingly brings home to the audience not only the savagery of Regan and Cornwall, but the general state of anarchy largely resulting from Lear's distortion of the social order by his abdication.

Hang . . . eyes The savagery of the sisters, now unbridled by diplomacy, succinctly revealed.

where To whom.

festinate Rapid.

posts Messengers.

intelligent Communicate.

Hot questrists Urgent seekers.

pass . . . life Condemn him to death.

do a court'sy to our wrath Indulge.

corky Shrivelled (with age).

as you . . . none I'm as innocent as you are guilty.

to pluck me . . . An especially contemptuous insult.

Naughty Wicked.

favours Features.

simple-answer'd Honest.

footed Landed.

the lunatic King Note how Regan speaks of him in the third person.

guessingly . . . down Tentatively written.

tied Like a bear, tied to be baited by dogs.

course Groups of dogs.

Rash Slash.

stelled Starry.

Holp Helped – by weeping himself. Gloucester here reverses the image: whereas the stormy sea would have risen up and quenched the stars, Lear wept.

dearn Dreary.

All . . . subscribe All other cruel creatures (like wolves) yield – and would have yielded in such a night – to compassion. The implication is that Regan, being crueller, did not.

winged Divine.

th'other too i.e. the other eye.

you i.e. Gloucester. This is a taunting prelude to the blinding.

a beard The servant echoes Regan, perhaps unwittingly. He hints at her leading role in this cruelty. Does he imply she has corrupted Cornwall?

villain Serf.

take . . . anger Take the chance of fighting in anger.

sparks of nature Sources of good feeling.

quit Pay off.

made . . . overture Revealed.

Kind Gods The adjective is not ironic: Gloucester is beseeching the Gods to be kind to Edgar.

Untimely At a bad time i.e. when they are preparing for battle.

I'll never . . . him Like Edgar at the end of the previous scene, the two servants act as a chorus.

Revision questions on Act III

1 'I will be the pattern of all patience.' Give examples of Lear's efforts to be patient in Acts II and III.

2 What other new aspect of Lear's character is revealed in Act III? Show how it is revealed.

3 How does Shakespeare achieve the effect of intense pathos in the storm scenes?

4 Discuss the effect of the scraps of song in the play.

5 Comment on the structure of this act, scene by scene.

Act IV Scene 1

Edgar meets Gloucester, led by an old man, and helps him on his way to Dover. The old earl is helped by the child he rejected, just as Lear is cared for by Cordelia.

Commentary

Observe Shakespeare's neglect of realism here in the interests of dramatic suspense and intensity: against all instinct Edgar maintains his disguise, giving rise to a series of painful ironies (for which, see notes on the scene). This episode is crucial: in the enlightenment of Gloucester which results from his blinding we see the coming together of the symbolic and the realistic elements in the play in the most dramatic way.

Yet better . . . Edgar is, as it were, continuing the meditations we left him with at the end of II, 6. Here he reaches the conclusion that things always get better in the end – ironically premature in view of Gloucester's entrance at IV, 1, 10.

Yet . . . worst It is better to be condemned and know it, than to be so and not to know it.

Fortune Fortune is one pole of Shakespeare's moral universe: the other is nature. Both are aspects of necessity. Our own distinction between environment and heredity is comparable.

Stands . . . esperance Is still able to hope.

poorly led Literally 'led by a peasant' – but with overtones of having appallingly come down in the world.

mutations Changes of circumstance.

Life . . . age We only resign ourselves to growing old because of the distressing mutability of things. Edgar's growing optimism has been cut brutally short.

I have no way Learning of Edmund's deceit has made Gloucester lose his moral bearings, like Lear.

Our means . . . commodities Our resources make us secure, but our defects prove advantages – by making us careful and self-aware.

Edgar Gloucester cannot know that Edgar is by him – a fine example of dramatic irony used for pathos.

This is the worst i.e. while we can say such things, the worst cannot yet have come.

My son Shakespeare commonly uses unlikely non-recognition of parents and children in thin disguises.

As flies . . . sport The irony is complex. Gloucester wishes to find Edgar: he has, but doesn't know it. His description of fate here is appropriate to his feeling; later, he recovers from complete despair, yet these lines reverberate through the play as one way of summing up the nature of things which is not finally denied or confirmed.

How . . . be? The question may apply to Gloucester's mental and physical state, or to his forgiveness.

Bad . . . sorrow It is a bad thing to play the fool before such a grieving man. Yet Edgar goes on and does it, because he must if the scene at Dover is to take place. Shakespeare skates over an awkwardness here: the audience wonders why Edgar does not reveal himself, in view of his feeling about deceit. At this point dramatic necessity takes precedence over realism.

the times' plague Gloucester sees his own predicament as symptomatic: Regan and Goneril are 'mad'.

daub it Keep up the deception.

Obidicut etc More names of fiends.

mopping and mowing Making faces.

all strokes Accept all that happens.

that I . . . happier Gloucester means that he has given Edgar money to lead him: this should make him happier. But his words ironically echo Edgar's soliloquy in III, 6: far from the grief of this great one making life easier for those below, it intensifies Edgar's own misery.

superfluous Indulged.

slaves your ordinance Treats your commands with contempt.

see . . . feel Now Gloucester cannot see he has learnt to feel. Compare these lines with Lear's comment on the need to blot out excessive feeling by bodily suffering (III, 4, 8–16).

So . . . enough Like Lear, Gloucester has been brought by his suffering to social insights, among others. If we could truly feel for the deprivation of others, we would act on our feelings to distribute our excess.

confined deep The sea restrained by the cliffs.

repair Reward.

Act IV Scene 2

Accompanied by Edmund, Goneril arrives outside her palace, surprised that her husband, Albany, has not come out to meet her. Before Edmund leaves she gives him clear signs of her affection, and hints that if he is ready to dispose of Albany, she will gladly take him as her husband. Albany then enters: he has thought more about Lear's condition and blames his wife for her treatment of the king. She dismisses his protests with contempt, having already shown that she thinks Albany weak.

A messenger then enters with the news of Cornwall's death and the narrative of Gloucester's blinding, which confirms Albany's fears. Goneril is worried that Cornwall's death will give her sister an advantage with Edmund.

Commentary

The scene shows the beginning of a rift between the two sisters, which is to culminate in the poisoning of Regan by Goneril; and it also confirms Albany in opposition to his wife, whom he addresses in language reminiscent of Lear's in I, 4.

sot Idiot. Albany's doubts are growing.

turn'd . . . out Misinterpreted the circumstances.

cowish Cowardly.

he'll . . . answer He'll overlook wrongs which might require action. Goneril's contempt makes her judge unfairly, as we see in Act V.

wishes i.e. that we (Goneril and Edmund) might become lovers.

prove effects Be granted.

brother Cornwall.

change Exchange.

distaff Spinning stick – the symbol of womanhood, as the sword was of manhood. Goneril will take her husband's sword.

mistress's A macabre play on words: Goneril will be Edmund's love – and she will also instruct him to dispose of Albany.

Would . . . well There are sexual allusions here to erection and conception.

Yours . . . death Edmund pledges his loyal military service to Goneril – but 'death' was also contemporary slang for orgasm.

A fool i.e. Albany.

worth the whistle i.e. in the past Albany would have made haste to meet her. He takes up her words, already disillusioned with his wife.

origin i.e. Lear.

border'd . . . itself Kept within set bounds i.e. is uncontrollable.

sliver and disbranch Both meaning 'tear off'.

material sap Essential food.

Filths . . . themselves The filthy can taste only themselves.

Tigers Albany sustains the wild animal imagery (see 'bear' below).

head-lugg'd Pulled by the head i.e. referring to a bear on a chain.

Thine . . . suffering What can be accepted with honour from what must be avenged.

Fools i.e. only fools.

villains Such as Lear, who has been 'punished' and is probably in league with France to make trouble for Goneril and Albany.

noiseless The land is noiseless because no preparations for war have been made – preparations signalled by beating drums.

plumed helm i.e. military dress.

Proper Appropriate i.e. to the fiend but not to woman.

self-cover'd Goneril has indeed changed from the woman he first knew – because her real self has now emerged: it is with this she is covered, and which be-monsters her face.

blood Instinct. Albany used the word in its usual sense in this play: proper feeling. Interestingly, he indicates here that another proper feeling – respect for woman – conflicts with and overrides the first.

howe'er But although.

mew! Goneril implies that Albany has no manhood, by making cat noises.

thrill'd Moved.

bending Turning.

widow i.e. Regan. These are Goneril's private thoughts.

pluck Bring down.

hateful i.e. life will be hateful if Regan steps in and deprives her of Edmund.

Ay This news confirms Albany in his determination to stand firm against the wickedness of the sisters.

Act IV Scene 3

In the French camp near Dover, Kent hears about the impression his letters have made on Cordelia. We discover that Lear is in Dover but is too ashamed to communicate with Cordelia.

Commentary

Cordelia's loving kindness is made clear in a vital way: she has been long absent from the play, and Shakespeare needs to bring out the contrast with her sisters vividly. He does so in a way which makes us forget to question the credibility of the idea that Kent has had time to write letters. The gentleman's description is also useful to a character who is defined by not being able to describe her own virtues.

imperfect Unfinished.

trill'd Trickled.

rebel-like But Cordelia, unlike her father and sisters, is able to master this passion.

express . . . goodliest Make her appear most beautiful.

those happy smilets Shakespeare takes trouble to distinguish Cordelia sharply from her sisters. Compare these lines with the recent description of Goneril IV, 2, 62–3.

If all . . . it If it made others as beautiful as it made her.

Sisters . . . it! Grief makes Cordelia almost as incoherent as Lear.

clamour moisten'd Calmed her passion by weeping.

started Went (abruptly).

It is the stars Kent takes up Gloucester's theme I, 2, 100–115. His point is that parents alone could not give characters to children so different as Cordelia and her sisters.

better tune Sane moments.

What . . . about i.e. that Cordelia and France shall save him from Regan and Goneril.

elbows Jogs his elbow.

casualties Hazards.

dog-hearted Cruel.

grieve . . . acquaintance Regret having known me.

Act IV Scene 4

Cordelia appears for the first time since I, 1, asks anxiously after her father, and sends her people in search of him. A messenger comes with news of the British army's advance, and Cordelia declares that she is prepared.

Commentary

This scene prepares us for the meeting between Lear and his youngest daughter. We find her ready not only to forgive but to overlook.

the vex'd sea The imagery of the sea runs throughout the play though, like Gloucester, we never come near the thing itself. In Shakespeare's work generally it is a symbol for Fortune and Providence – unpredictable, all-powerful.

rank fumiter Lush fumitory – a herb much grown in Shakespeare's time.

century Hundred soldiers – or any large body of men.

can Knows.

bereaved Damaged.

simples Healing herbs.

aidant Helpful.

importun'd Importunate. She means that her husband – the king of France – has been moved to send an army by her tears and grief.

blown Proud.

love An appropriate remark for one motivated throughout by love.

Act IV Scene 5

Oswald has arrived at Gloucester's castle with a letter from Goneril to Edmund. Edmund, however, has set out to find and kill Gloucester. Regan, suspecting what is in her sister's letter, asks Oswald to let her see it, but he refuses. This provokes her into the assertion that now Cornwall is dead she is more available to Edmund than Goneril is, and she instructs Oswald to tell her sister this.

Oswald goes out after Edmund, to give him the letter, saying that if he meets Gloucester he will gladly despatch the earl himself.

Commentary

Ironically, Regan seals her own doom by her outburst to Oswald. Her selfish desires are sharply contrasted with Cordelia's selfless love. Regan's lust is an example of what Lear rages against in IV, 6, 108–31.

brother Albany.

ado Trouble. Albany is reluctant.

pity of his misery This of course is ironic.

nighted Darkened – because blinded. Regan cannot know how it is
  spiritually darkened also.
descry Spy out.
I know not what Regan suspects Goneril, as Goneril suspected her.
œilliads Amorous looks.
I . . . understanding I know what I'm talking about.
call Recall. Regan does not specify what Goneril's 'wisdom' is – perhaps the
  knowledge that her husband still lives. If so, she underestimates her sister.

Act IV Scene 6

This scene falls into three distinct parts.
1) Edgar, as poor Tom, leads Gloucester to the supposed edge of a
cliff, and when he throws himself down on flat ground persuades
him, in the character of a peasant beneath Dover cliff, that he has
jumped down the fearful cliff and been miraculously preserved
from death by the gods.
2) Lear, fantastically dressed with wild flowers, meets Gloucester,
and the two victims of plot and sub-plot are thus on the stage
together. The Gentleman sent by Cordelia to find Lear here comes
upon him, and Edgar learns from him that a battle is imminent.
3) As the Gentleman finds Lear, so Oswald comes across Gloucester, but is prevented from killing him by Edgar, who kills Oswald.
Before he dies Oswald implores Edgar to give the letters about him
to 'Edmund, Earl of Gloucester'.
  Edgar opens a letter from Goneril to Edmund, inviting him to kill
Albany and take the duke's place as her husband. Edgar keeps the
letter to show to the duke.

Commentary

This scene strikingly comprises the extremes of Shakespeare's
dramatic method: on the one hand the simple melodrama associated with Oswald, on the other the symbolic dimensions of Gloucester's imagined suicide and his meeting with Lear. Without
inhibition the playwright mingles the mundane and the poetic,
carrying forward the plots while exploring the progress through the
suffering of Lear and Gloucester. As Gloucester recovers from one
fit of suicidal 'madness' he encounters the truly mad Lear.

How fearful Edgar paints a picture of the place, both for the blind
  Gloucester and for the audience.
choughs Jackdaws.

midway air i.e. between Gloucester and the sea.

bark Boat.

cock Dinghy.

the deficient . . . headlong I, because of deficient sight, fall.

leap upright i.e. because even that would throw him over.

Why I do trifle . . . In retrospect this legitimates Edgar's continued disguise. One cannot suppose he thought out the plan at once, however.

fall Begin.

snuff Used candle-wick – therefore the useless remnant of his life.

conceit . . . theft Imagination may deprive a man of life when he wants to die. Edgar is worried that the combination of shock and the desire for suicide may in fact kill Gloucester, when Edgar's plan is that his apparently providential recovery will make him want to live.

shiver'd Shattered.

at each End to end.

bourn Boundary i.e. cliff.

gorg'd Throated.

the tyrant Wretchedness.

whelk'd Swollen.

them . . . impossibilities Honours for themselves by doing things men cannot.

The . . . thus Sanity will not equip its possessor like this.

coining Minting money – which was the king's prerogative.

Nature's . . . respect Born a king, Lear cannot be deprived of his rights. The sequence of his thoughts is often difficult to follow now that Lear has been engulfed by insanity, but he alludes to all the play's themes.

press-money Money for conscripts 'pressed' into service.

crow-keeper Scarecrow.

clothier's yard An arrow was the length of a cloth-yard.

bills Halberdiers.

clout Bull's-eye.

hewgh! The sound of the arrow. The whole speech revolves about archery.

white hairs . . . there i.e. he had the white hairs of wisdom even before he grew a beard. The speech is concerned with forms of flattery. Lear is not so mad that he does not know them for what they were.

I found 'em i.e. because the rain, wind and thunder proved the flatterers wrong. The obvious parallel is with Canute.

trick Distinguishing characteristic.

Ay, every inch . . . This speech establishes the link between lechery and injustice explored here and in lines 154–71. While the associations are complex the fundamental notion is simple: both lechery and injustice spring from the corruption of the passions by lust of various kinds. Lear is much concerned with such lust – for power, for flesh – recognizing it in his daughters, though not yet in himself. But the imagery links their cruelty and lechery with his own initial injustice which unleashed these passions.

cause Crime.

Gloucester's . . . son Lear does not know about Edmund.

Luxury Lechery.

For . . . soldiers Lear links his deprivation with lechery.

Whose . . . snow Who appears to be virtuous.

forks Legs.

minces virtue Pretends to chastity and innocence.

fitchew Pole-cat.

soiled Freshly fed (and therefore frisky).

Centaurs Centaurs in pagan literature were half human, half horse.

girdle Waist. Only that part of the centaur (or woman) above the waist is divine – the rest fiendish.

civet Used for making perfume.

eyes Lear's cruel references are no doubt prompted by Gloucester's bandages.

blind Cupid Cupid, the god of love, was traditionally represented as blind. But in the 16th century the image also indicated a brothel.

my heart breaks This is one of the play's climactic moments, as the two shattered fathers encounter one another, one physically blind, the other mentally.

case Sockets.

heavy case Bad way. Shakespeare habitually makes such puns at moments of great pathos.

feelingly Gloucester puns on the two meanings acutely, and with feeling. Lear takes up the paradox 'look with thine ears' in his next speech.

simple Peasant.

change places Lear pursues the theme of the hypocrisy in hierarchy – which is not to say that Shakespeare condemns such hierarchy. As the clothes imagery shows in his next speech, the point is rather that kings and judges should not be fooled by their fine robes into thinking themselves better than other men. Lear has fallen into the trap of confusing his royal status with his human condition: that has led him seriously astray.

handy-dandy Take your pick – from a children's game.

creature Man.

Authority Authority – parental and political, human and divine – is a fundamental theme of the play.

cozener Petty conman. The judge who sentences him, says Lear, is guilty of usury – earning interest on his money – and so no better than he.

able Authorize.

who i.e. Lear, who has the money to bribe the accuser.

politician Schemer.

matter and impertinency Sense and irrelevance.

Reason in madness This phrase sums up Lear's thematic and symbolic – as opposed to his dramatic – significance in these scenes. On the dramatic level he is a man sinking into madness: thematically he gives expression to the play's larger issues.

a good block Lear is diverted from his theme by noticing the hat he holds – the hat being formed on a block and made of felt.

delicate Ingenious.

kill Notice the rapid transitions of sense and mood in these speeches, as Lear passes from meditation – almost addressing himself – through abrupt associations of ideas, almost to hysteria.

natural . . . Fortune Born to be the plaything of Fortune.

cut to th'brains Mad. But we may also imagine Lear touching his head here, and thinking of a wound.

No seconds? No one else?

salt Tears.

bravely A pun: 'with courage' and 'finely-dressed'.

smug Well-groomed.

there's life in't There's still hope.

in a King The notion of royal dignity is strong in Shakespeare.

gentle Noble.

sure and vulgar Certain and well-known.

main . . . thought We expect the main army to come into view at any moment.

worser spirit Bad angel – which tempted him to suicide.

by . . . sorrows Taught by the experience of deeply-felt sorrows.

pregnant Susceptible.

benison Blessing.

To boot Into the bargain i.e. together with Gloucester's thanks.

A proclaim'd prize! i.e. one who has been publicly declared an outlaw – and therefore with a price on his head.

thyself remember i.e. in order to confess your sins before death – a Christian oversight in a pagan play.

friendly i.e. because Gloucester still really desires death.

to't To the sword.

Chill I'll. Edgar assumes another disguise, that of a yokel.

'casion Cause.

go your gait Go on your way.

And 'chud ha' If I could.

che vor' ye I warn you.

costard Head. Literally an apple.

ballow Stick.

dunghill Guttersnipe.

foins Thrusts – fencing: Oswald has a sword against Edgar's stick.

the letters Edgar's reading of the letters is part of Edmund's undoing.

Upon Among.

serviceable Active – in the sense of 'ready to serve both others' and your own interests.

deathsman Executioner.

manners i.e. good manners, which condemn opening the letters of others.

cut him off Kill him i.e. Albany.

labour i.e. of making love. Goneril and Edmund persistently communicate in barely-veiled double entendres. The irony is that as Edmund trapped Edgar with a forged letter, so Edmund himself is caught by the genuine article.

O . . . will! O the unlimited extent of women's desires!

upon Against.

rake up Cover over. They are not, of course, really on the beach: for once Shakespeare is consistent.

mature Appropriate.

ungracious Evil.

death-practis'd Whose murder was plotted.

stiff Sturdy.

vile i.e. because they still let him feel his misery.

ingenious Sensitive.

wrong imaginations Hallucinations. Madness, like bodily suffering, is seen to be a deadener of grief.

Act IV Scene 7

Kent has brought Lear to the French camp where Cordelia and the doctor wait for the king to regain consciousness. He does so slowly, uncertain of where or what he is. His restoration to sanity is accompanied by music, often the sign of healing in Shakespeare. The scene ends with a choral exchange between Kent and a gentleman about the imminent battle between the armies of France and Britain.

Commentary

Lear's madness has passed, but he is worn out by it. Our hopes are raised by the assumption that his troubles are over – only to be ironically dashed, by the result of the battle. This is the first exchange between Lear and Cordelia since her banishment and the first in which we see their mutual natural affection.

fail Because Kent's goodness cannot be measured or matched.

go with Conform to.

clipp'd Over-condensed.

weeds Garments.

memories Reminders.

my made intent The plan I intended.

boon Favour.

wind up Bring back into tune.

child-changed Either 'changed to a child' or 'changed by his children'.

I'th'sway According to the direction.

white flakes White hairs.

Challenge Lay claim to.

dread-bolted With dreaded thunder-bolts.

perdu Lost one.

helm Helmet i.e. of hair.

fain Obliged.

hovel thee Share a hovel.

short and musty Bitty and smelly.

wheel of fire Lear imagines he has died and is in hell.

wide Straying (in his mind).

abus'd Deceived. He means that he doesn't know what to believe.

fond Doting. Ironically, in his moment of self-recognition, Lear comes round to the view of himself promoted by Goneril and Regan. But notice the beautiful balance and clarity of this speech, after his ravings.

mainly Completely.

my child The first of two moments in the play when a 'true' parent and child discover one another. For the other see V, 3, 159.

even o'er Recollect.

Till further settling Until he is more tranquil.

old . . . Lear now harps on this point, as he did before on his pride: old habits die hard.

conductor General.

Revision questions on Act IV

1 Illustrate how one of the effects of Gloucester's suffering is to make him think of others in distress, even as Lear did.

2 Contrast the attitudes of Goneril and Albany to the danger of foreign invasion.

3 What is the *dramatic* reason for the return of the King of France to his own country?

4 What is shown (*a*) of Regan's character, (*b*) of Oswald's, when they meet in this act?

5 'Lear misunderstood all his daughters, but none so much as Cordelia.' Illustrate this statement from the two scenes in which she appears in this act.

Act V Scene 1

Regan anxiously questions Edmund about whether he prefers her sister to her. When Goneril enters with Albany she shows the same eagerness to secure Edmund. Albany, who takes the lead in the battle, makes it clear that while he will fight the invading French army he will not penalize Lear and Cordelia. Edgar, approaching in disguise, hands him the letter Goneril wrote to

Edmund – the letter he took from Oswald – and asks Albany to read it later. The scene ends with Edmund's consideration of his position in relation to the two sisters. He decides that the best thing is to wait until after the battle, and then take whichever of the two will dispose of Albany, so making Edmund effective king.

Commentary

This scene concentrates on the sub-plot. Juxtaposition with IV, 7 highlights the difference between Cordelia and her sisters, between love and lust. But the important focus is on Edmund and the contrast between his calculation of advantage and Cordelia's readiness to give all. Albany's role as a man of some substance emerges decisively, preparing the way for his ordering of events in V, 3.

Know Enquire.

last purpose Most recent decision.

advis'd by aught Persuaded by anything.

self-reproving Self-doubt. Edmund paints a vivid and contemptuous picture of Albany, a good man struggling with his conscience.

constant pleasure Settled intention.

man i.e. Oswald.

miscarried Come to grief.

intend Intend to confer.

forfended Forbidden.

conjunct Joined.

bosom'd Intimate.

as far . . . hers As far as it is possible to be i.e. sexually.

She and the Duke Goneril enters at a charged moment.

loosen Part. Sexual desire is taking over from the lust for power as the dominant motive in the sisters.

loving Ironic, in view of what has just passed. Doubly ironic, in that Regan wants to keep him alive only to tie down Goneril.

Not . . . King Obscure. Albany appears to be saying that the business is serious not because France supports Lear and other malcontents, but by virtue of the very fact that he has invaded. In other words, he is trying to detach Lear from legitimate objections to the King of France's invasion.

nobly Knowing Edmund, we understand the irony here.

reason'd Discussed. Like his wife, Regan regards Albany as a talker, when he should be a doer.

particular broils Private disputes.

th'ancient of war Those experienced in war.

I know the riddle Goneril understands that Regan is trying to keep her apart from Edmund.

avouched Asserted.

machination Plotting.

serve suit.

urged Edmund pushes Albany.

greet the time Take things as they come. Albany is putting Edmund down.

jealous Mistrustful. Edmund's imagery and extrovert manner are typical of his approach to life. The slightly melodramatic style – reminiscent of the presentation of Iago in Othello – is well suited to this dynamic, crude over-reacher.

carry . . . side Get what I want.

taking off Murder.

my state . . . defend It is up to me to look after my power. Taken with the rest of line 69, this can also mean: my task is to get on with things, not to talk about them.

Act V Scene 2

Lear and Cordelia lose the battle while Gloucester is waiting under a tree, put there by the still disguised Edgar, who hastily returns to take him away. Gloucester once again loses heart, but Edgar urges him on.

Commentary

It is not clear why Edgar still conceals his identity, though the concealment certainly prolongs the symbolic strength of a situation in which a blind man is led by a mad beggar. Gloucester's ignorance of the beggar's true identity emphasizes the strength of his renewed resolve, which is not helped by personal affection.

comfort Help. This is ironic: the revelation that his saviour is Edgar kills Gloucester.

Ripeness Preparation. These stoical lines are central to the play, encapsulating the attitude towards which Gloucester and Lear advance. Whether they reach it is a debatable point.

Act V Scene 3

Lear and Cordelia appear as Edmund's prisoners, but both of them are completely happy. After they have been taken away under guard, Edmund gives secret orders for their death.

Albany then appears with Goneril and Regan, and after some bickering between the two sisters concerning their right to Edmund, Albany proclaims Edmund a traitor and announces

that if no one appears on the sound of the trumpet to make
good this charge, Albany will do so himself in single combat.
The trumpet sounds and, as he had promised, Edgar comes
forward, disguised now in armour. He fights Edmund and
wounds him mortally. Meanwhile Regan has been taken ill –
poisoned by Goneril. Albany produces his wife's incriminating
letter. After attempting to seize it she rushes out and commits
suicide.

On his death-bed Edmund repents and tells his story. Then
Edgar narrates the death of Gloucester. Edmund suddenly
remembers his instructions concerning Lear and Cordelia, and a
messenger is sent to reprieve them, but he arrives too late to save
Cordelia. Lear carries in her body and soon dies of grief. Albany
then offers the kingdom to Kent, but he refuses it, sensing his
own imminent death, and it is left to Edgar and Albany to pick
up the pieces.

Commentary

A complex scene in which plot and sub-plot are again brought
together, as Shakespeare goes through the usual business of
tying up the ends. Central are the deaths of Cordelia (offstage)
and Lear (on) which give a further twist to the tragic screw,
forcing the audience to revise any conclusions they may have
reached and speculate further on the play's significance. Everything else, including Edmund's unlikely conversion, forms a
backdrop for these casually introduced events. Up to the very
end of the play Shakespeare manifests his delight in the theatrical, even the melodramatic, as the duel, the incriminating letter,
Edmund's repentance and Lear's great final entrance show.

their Albany and the sisters.
best meaning Best intention. Notice Cordelia's rhyming couplets: they
  give her words a formal, authoritative quality.
No, no Lear is transformed. This is his brief moment of content.
wear out Outlast.
packs and sects Confederacies and cliques.
ebb . . . moon Go quickly out and in (like the tide). Lear's images
  contrast the implied strength of their love with the inconstancy of
  human life. His references to court life show how detached he now is
  from the world he once dominated.
caught Either 'understood' or 'Is this really you?'
fire Drive us with fire.
good years Meaning uncertain. This may mean that the years of their

stolen prosperity will nevertheless bring them, like everything else, to final judgement.

flesh and fell flesh and skin i.e. completely.

men . . . is A perfect expression of Edmund's view: he means that, to do well, men *should* adapt themselves to circumstances. This contrasts sharply with what we have just heard from Lear.

sword Soldier.

Will . . . question Is not for discussion.

carry . . . down Do it according to my instructions.

I . . . do't Ironic. The officer says he is not an animal but a human being, yet the task he agrees to fulfil is worse than bestial: animals do not kill for profit. This continues the play's insistent comparisons of human and animal life.

strain Temperament.

Fortune It is appropriate to invoke Fortune as Edmund's patroness. Very soon she will desert him.

retention Detention.

Whose i.e. the king's.

pluck . . . bosom Gain the affection of the people.

impress'd lances Conscripts.

on . . . them On us who command them.

quarrels Cases.

sharpness Wrongness. Edmund argues that Lear and Cordelia will be unfairly judged in the hot aftermath of the battle. As with his father, he appears plausible.

list Please.

Bore . . . person Took on the authority of my role (as queen) and person (being present at the battle).

immediacy Position of immediate authority i.e. not a mere delegate.

hot Quick.

In . . . grace On his own account.

addition Titles.

compeers Is equal to. Goneril wishes to make Edmund dependent on her; Regan wants to establish his freedom.

husband Marry. Albany is being ironic – he has read Edgar's letter.

That . . . a-squint You don't know what you're talking about. Notice how the sisters soon descend to bickering.

full-flowing stomach With all the force of my anger.

walls Like a conquered town, Regan is vanquished by Edmund.

let-alone Refusal.

Half-blooded Bastard.

reason Both 'what is just' and 'the cause'.

capital Punishable by death.

attaint Impeachment.

gilded This can mean 'bloody' or 'superficially attractive' – in the context, possibly both.

banes Banns.

An interlude! A play! Goneril speaks sarcastically.

upon i.e. by fighting.

heart Blood. Albany means that he will prove Edmund's treason by defeating him in single combat.

medicine Ironic to the last, Goneril means poison.

On him . . . not? Against anyone at all.

single virtue Power alone.

Edgar, armed Edgar appears in yet another disguise.

canker-bit Worm-eaten.

cope Meet.

privilege i.e. to do battle with an equal.

honours Knighthood.

profession Affirmation of the oath of knighthood.

Maugre Despite.

upward Top. This flowery language is usual in challenges.

descent Very bottom.

toad-spotted As treacherous as the toad is spotted.

In wisdom Edmund was bound to fight only an equal in rank.

delay Decline.

Back . . . The exchange of insults is conventional.

shall . . . way Will dispose of them at once.

practice Plotting.

cozen'd and beguil'd Cheated and tricked.

stople Stop.

No tearing Desperate, Goneril tries to destroy the paper.

the laws are mine This perfectly expresses Goneril's whole life, and shows her a true child of her father as he was: arbitrary and violent.

fortune on Victory over.

Let's . . . charity Let's forgive each other.

dark . . . place The adulterer's bed. The echo of Lear's earlier speeches here reveals Edgar in yet another role: the mouthpiece of the avenging furies.

'tis true Note the abruptness of Edmund's change of heart on his deathbed.

gait Bearing.

List Listen. Shakespeare gives Edgar a narrative which fills in Gloucester's last hours. Notice the involved syntax and broken sentences, suggesting the strength of Edgar's grief. But notice also the way Shakespeare gives the character yet another role, as the action stops for a moment, Edmund pauses in his dying, and he tells the story.

hourly Hour after hour. We would rather live to imagine death again and again, than be caught and killed.

O fault! Edgar here confirms our doubts.

You look . . . This is a strange request from Edmund.

dissolve Weep.

a period Enough.

big in clamour Noisily grief-stricken.

came there in a man Shakespeare is tying up all the ends before launching into the final climax.

puissant Strong.

tranc'd Insensible.

in disguise Note the parallelism between Edgar and Kent.

improper Unsuitable.

Help . . . After the lull of Edgar's speeches, the tension is suddenly cranked up again.

judgment . . . heavens Albany constantly invokes the gods and heaven.

compliment Proper observances.

object i.e. the bodies of Goneril and Regan.

fordid Killed.

promis'd end Last Judgment. We noted earlier how the play's references extend its scope from a bloody local scrimmage to a universalized catastrophe. This habit is typical of tragedy. Edgar's comment is more accurate.

Fall and cease The heavens should fall, and the world end. Albany's hyperbole is characteristic of Shakespeare's attempt to give poetic expression to the occasion's horror.

Prithee away Lear is now indifferent to everything except Cordelia – extreme as always, he turns to violence when sympathy is offered.

falchion Sword.

One of them i.e. Lear. Kent may mean the other one to be himself – or perhaps Cordelia.

dull Sad.

first Start.

difference and decay Alteration and failing fortune.

fordone Destroyed. This is not quite accurate. Goneril killed Regan.

so I think Lear replies vacantly. He isn't listening.

bootless Useless.

great decay i.e. Lear.

boot Reward.

fool Innocent i.e. Cordelia.

dog . . . rat The play's final animal comparison.

Never . . . A famous line in which the one word is reiterated to extraordinary and powerful effect – very much an actor's line, for everything depends upon intonation.

undo this button Lear feels the choking of death and takes it for tight clothes.

Look there As he dies, it seems Lear believes Cordelia to be alive.

tough Harsh.

gor'd Torn.

a journey i.e. to death.

My master It is not clear whether Kent means Lear, or the king of the gods.

what we feel These words return us to an early theme of the play: the distinction between truthful feeling and its expression, and deceiving.

Revision questions on Act V

1 Give illustrations of Edmund's deceit in this act.

2 Contrast the battle scene with any other of which you know in Shakespeare. Do you find the one in this play convincing?

3 In what way does Albany appear a different man from the Albany of Act I?

4 'An interlude!' What occasioned this exclamation by Goneril (Scene 3)?

5 Comment on the extreme pathos of the last part of the play, between Lear's entrance with Cordelia dead in his arms and his own death. How is this pathos achieved – or emphasized – dramatically?

26131

Shakespeare's art in *King Lear*
King Lear and the nature of tragedy

Realism and tragedy

To say that *King Lear* is the least realistic of Shakespeare's major tragedies is not to say that it is unrealistic – commentators have testified to the authenticity of Lear's madness, for example – but that its realism is subordinated to another purpose: the examination by symbolic means of fundamental questions about the nature of man and his existence. These are questions which philosophers and theologians have tried to answer. Tragedy is a means of asking them in a peculiarly intense way.

Shakespeare's Elizabethan predecessors had moralized their tragedy, making it illustrate certain ethical conclusions. Shakespeare himself goes beyond this didactic purpose into an exploration of the validity of all moral values. In *King Lear* everything is tested. The tragedy of manners found in Marlowe and Kyd is superseded by a poetic drama in which the layers of behaviour and circumstance are stripped away, so that we are forced to ask ourselves whether there is any human essence left when every hope, every dignity is removed from an individual. This is the meaning of Lear's final trial, when Cordelia is killed before his eyes. Does anything then remain to him? It is this question which Shakespeare puts not only in the form of action – or rather, a series of actions – but through the reflections of the various characters in the play and the images they use. This is what is meant by calling the play a poetic drama rather than a primarily realistic one: it uses language which cannot finally be translated back into terms of the obvious or everyday.

In one sense, of course, we might want to say that this makes his work more 'realistic' than Marlowe's or Kyd's, in that he recognizes and records a wider domain of experience than they do. In this respect *King Lear* is a more sympathetic play than Marlowe's *Dr Faustus*, for example, in which a religious and moral framework is clearly defined. The central character of Shakespeare's tragedy is confused, even unto death: he does not experience even Hamlet's or Macbeth's final bleak enlightenment. We are left to ponder on his plight. This is an aspect of the play which encourages us to refrain from making up our minds about what it all means, remaining instead in a state of fruitful uncertainty.

Such a tendency is encouraged further by the complex verbal texture of Shakespeare's verse. Like all the other great plays, *King Lear* has been found to have a complex network of images and allusions which turn our attention aside from the action itself to consider its significance. Given that Lear himself is an unreflective character who is forced by circumstances to reflect on his predicament (and Gloucester is similarly placed) the whole play urges us away from a mere acceptance of the events at face value towards the notion that they mean something else. If this is always true of Shakespeare it is especially true of *King Lear*. If we call it a play about a silly old man who messes up his life, we hardly say enough! As a consequence, the work has been subject to endless interpretation and reinterpretation.

Interpretations

In the late 17th century Nahum Tate adapted the play for the taste of his time. Tate explains in his introduction that he wishes to make the story more credible. He therefore makes Cordelia and Edgar lovers and brings Lear and his daughter to a happy ending. While acknowledging Shakespeare's 'Creating Fancy' Tate found the play 'a Heap of Jewels, unstrung and unpolished' – in other words, incoherent. His age had a preference for simplicity and unity, symmetry and order. He made the play into what he saw as a more realistic drama, and in this version it held the stage until the actor Macready restored something like the original text in 1838. Even when this was done, the general opinion in the 19th century shared the previous era's view that the play was great but unactable because it was so incredible. Samuel Johnson had found Shakespeare's ending unbearably painful to read. He felt it a mistake to show virtue suffering at the end. Whereas the 18th century saw tragedy essentially in moral terms, for the 19th century the play was a great spiritual odyssey. But both views – the moral and the spiritual – found difficulty in accommodating the end of the play. Lear's final speech is ambiguous. Does he die thinking Cordelia still lives – and therefore happy? Or does he realize she really is dead? Is he mad or sane? It may be that this is a detail and that what matters is that we, the audience, know she is dead, which makes the pathos of Lear's last words all the more painful. Certainly Cordelia's death represents an avoidance of the sort of poetic justice advocated by Tate and Johnson.

The violence and apparent cruelty of this ending have their

roots in a type of tragedy popular in Shakespeare's time, especially in translations of Seneca, the Roman playwright, whose works are full of blood and thunder. Whereas Aristotle had suggested catharsis as the focus of tragic experience, that purification which leaves the audience chastened and reflective, Senecan tragedy is designed to remind us that the world is a harsh and violent place and to acclimatize us to the fact. In both types of tragedy pride is humbled through hamartia – the tragic fault – but for different ends. Shakespeare follows neither view, though he borrows from both. The world of *King Lear* is indeed a savage place, its cruelty apparently incomprehensible, but there is no sense that the savagery is there to titillate or subdue the audience. Instead the violence underlines the questions asked in the play about the nature of man and his place in the scheme of things.

Tragedy and justice

This brings us to the question of whether, in *King Lear*, there *is* a scheme of things. The issue is much alluded to in the play; from Lear's first invocation to the sacred radiance of the sun, the play is filled with prayers, supplications and hints about a heavenly order (for more on this see the discussion of Gloucester). It is implied that the gods somehow control human life and that they dispense a kind of justice, inscrutable though it may be. Opinions vary. One common view seems to be Edgar's claim that: 'The Gods are just' (V, 3, 169). Yet as I have suggested in my discussion of Edgar, his conclusions throughout the play are usually invalidated by some immediately succeeding horror. This comment is no exception. Regan, Goneril and Edmund are dead or dying, Gloucester and Kent vindicated – when suddenly Albany remembers Lear, and he is brought in carrying the body of Cordelia. In short, whatever theories of divine justice are put forward they seem to be contradicted or qualified by the play's events.

The very evolution of tragedy, beginning with Aeschylus, is bound up with the notion of a universal justice. The tragic process is, in part, a righting of injustice. In the Revenge Tragedy, from which Shakespeare learnt so much, revenge figures as a primitive and personal exacting of this justice, sanctioned by Heaven. *King Lear* begins with an act of injustice – Lear's repudiation of Cordelia – and the repercussions of this act are felt throughout. When the storm breaks, Lear talks as though it were the result of divine intervention – but he sees it not as a punishment for himself but for Regan and Goneril:

> Let the great Gods,
> That keep this dreadful pudder o'er our heads,
> Find out their enemies now. (III, 2, 49–51)

This ironic misunderstanding shows the depth of Lear's self-deception. Again and again he refers to Heaven's justice, which he expects to be exacted in his own favour: 'And show the Heavens more just' (III, 4, 36). Later he stages a mock trial of Regan and Goneril (III, 6), ironic in view of the fact that the whole play constitutes his own trial. Only from IV, 6, with his outburst against those who can avoid justice because they 'Plate sin with gold' (163), does he begin to acknowledge, indirectly, his own former state. When he awakes from the sleep which ends his madness he tells Cordelia:

> I know you do not love me; for your sisters
> Have, as I do remember, done me wrong:
> You have some cause, they have not. (IV, 7, 73–5)

That 'some' is still a little grudging. Though the storm is over, the final reckoning is yet to come. Lear has begun to accept that inscrutable necessity which is the meaning of things, but there is one more test in store. Lear has been compared to Job – but Job, who suffered patiently, was rewarded by God. Lear is stripped of everything. What counts at the end is that he cares more for Cordelia than for himself – though that caring is still a faint reflection of the self-love which has not been purged from him, and which is expressed in ranting about his former self. In this respect he cannot reach the sombre pathos of Edgar's words:

> Men must endure
> Their going hence, even as their coming hither:
> Ripeness is all. (V, 2, 9–11)

although these lines echo Lear's own: 'Thou must be patient: we came crying hither . . .' (IV, 6, 176).

Whatever gods they may invoke, necessity is finally the 'divine' force which brings the characters in *King Lear* to heel – a necessity which seems to spring out of their own natures. Gloucester's references to the stars are as wide of the mark as Edmund's boastful claims to autonomy. The lesson seems to be that whatever forces there may be, we can only experience them in human life, and it is there we must learn how to live in justice and pity. When at the end Albany is told that Edmund has died he rightly says 'That's but a trifle here . . .' (V, 3, 294). No-one invokes the gods or speaks of justice after Lear's return. Only Kent and Edgar have a telling exchange:

Kent: Is this the promised end?
Edgar: Or image of that horror? (V, 3, 262–3)

They refer, of course, to the day of judgement, when all will be revealed and judged, and they see the end of the action as an image of that day – a day of horror. Justice is terrifying, not comforting, in its execution, even for those who are saved by it and have to watch. That is the grim note on which the play ends.

The characters

Lear

Who is it that can tell me who I am?

At least three of the important things about Lear – old age, parenthood and royal status – have nothing to do with what we normally call character but with his role in life: circumstances which bear on his character and put it under such stress that it disintegrates in a seeming chaos of self-doubt. It is, of course, impossible to separate role and character completely; if we think of role as largely determined by our relations with others, and character as our self perceived by others, they can be seen to merge into one another. But character can also be thought of as the self observing itself – not only as the product of our actions, outwardly demonstrated, but also as their source. I behave in the way I do because I see myself as a certain person, and my behaviour determines the way in which others see me – or so I would like to think. Usually there is a gap, wide or narrow, between these two conceptions of the self – my own and other people's – and it is this gap which especially interests Shakespeare in the tragedies. The questioning of identity, both personal and social, both character and role, is central to the great tragedies: *King Lear, Hamlet, Macbeth, Othello* and *Coriolanus*.

It might be said that the complete separation of what we are to ourselves from the way others see us is achieved only in madness; and many of the characters in the tragedies – not only the heroes – experience madness of some sort. This is a common phenomenon in Jacobean drama. In *King Lear* we see an old man who has been a king for many years: when he thinks of himself it is as a king that he does so – he calls himself a 'Dragon' (I, 1, 121) and owns up to his pride in royal honour (I, 1, 167–8). He has been absolute, used to obedience. Even as a parent he is a king (see I, 1). Lear confuses his parental and royal functions, expecting his daughters to flatter him like courtiers, and rewarding them in the manner of a monarch bestowing land on feudal vassals. It is left to France to make the point that this sort of dealing may be suitable in political life but not where personal relations are involved: 'Love's not love/When it is mingled with regards that stand/Aloof from the entire point.' (I, 1, 237–9).

Having identified his personality so completely with his royal role, Lear is thus especially vulnerable when he renounces the crown. Old age, loss of authority and personal cruelty are all waiting to torment him and bring his idea of himself into question. He is forced to reassess first his role – as a private citizen, newly subject to the whim of others, and as a formerly loved and loving father; then his character as a sane, rational man. Such is the stress he endures that Lear passes beyond even these painful enquiries to more fundamental metaphysical agonies about the very nature of his being. The questions what and who am I? may push the sane man into madness, or they may occur because of madness. In *King Lear* we find examples of both.

At the beginning of the play Shakespeare's first fine stroke is to bring us in at what promises to be the end of Lear's career. Feeling the onset of age, he has, with apparent wisdom, decided to renounce power. Yet ironically, it is in the ceremony of renunciation itself that his lack of wisdom is revealed. The Lear we see in I, 1 is proud and kingly, but also short-tempered, arbitrary, violent and irrational. In a short but telling coda to the scene, Regan and Goneril – who, for all their faults, are both perceptive and truthful about others – reveal that not only has Lear already started on the path to senility, but that his nature has always been rash and choleric. The crucial phrase here, foreshadowing the play's central preoccupation, is Regan's 'he hath ever but slenderly known himself' (I, 1, 292).

It appears in his treatment of Cordelia that Lear neither knows what he is nor what he wants. The two are distinguishable: it is only when Lear begins to discover what he really wants – not, for example, royal dignity or a hundred knights – that he has some intimation of what he is: 'a very foolish fond old man' (IV, 7, 60). In I, 1 he is far from such knowledge. Not only does he still speak as a king, but in the language of prices and property. Having 'invested' his love in Cordelia he is outraged when his capital shows no return, deciding that 'her price is fallen' (I, 1, 196). This is ironic for it is the value Lear unthinkingly sets on himself that is to be brought painfully into question. Cordelia, on the other hand, remains, in the words of one of Shakespeare's own sonnets, 'an ever-fixed mark'. Her abnegation of self contrasts powerfully with Lear's egocentricity, and the two are encapsulated in his complaint that she had better 'not been born than not t' have pleased me better' (I, 1, 233). The stress in that sentence is on the 'me'.

The note of petulance in this dismissal of Cordelia is sustained at the beginning of Act I, Scene 4, with Lear's first words: 'Let me not stay a jot for dinner: go, get it ready.' (I, 4, 8). Lear's impatience is kingly; but this trivial domestic request is to be the beginning of a revelation – that the king's writ no longer runs, even in the matter of dinner. Like ordinary mortals, Lear has to wait. Soon, he is suffering from the sort of insubordination from Goneril and her servant Oswald, he said in I, 1 he never could or would abide from anyone; and he is rapidly brought to questions about his identity. The speed with which Shakespeare achieves this transition – within the space of 350 lines – is breathtaking and characteristic of his extreme economy of means. The scene is worth some scrutiny.

Central to it are discussions about the nature of Authority, couched in different terms, according to who speaks. The scene begins with Kent, in disguise, being taken on as a servingman by Lear. In his plain speech Kent acknowledges Lear's royalty, and it is he who uses the key word: Authority (30) for what he finds in his master's face and bearing. Kent, in short, claims that Lear is naturally a king: it shows in his every move. The Fool takes a different view: devoted to the king, he still teaches him the lesson of his foolishness in renouncing his rightful authority. By doing this he has made himself 'an O without a figure' (I, 4, 189). Lear, while enjoying the Fool's banter, naturally prefers Kent's respect. Yet throughout the scene he is not quite in contact with either, preoccupied with his own discovery of neglect. This is indicated by Lear's intensifying sequence of questions about identity. This sequence begins at line 26 with an innocent – but in the circumstances ironic – enquiry of Kent: 'Dost thou know me, fellow?' It is, of course, Lear who does not know Kent – and therefore, by implication, himself. At line 78 the king haughtily asks of Oswald 'Who am I sir?' to be told that he is Goneril's father – an intolerable answer for one used to defining other people's existence in terms of his own. When at line 145 Lear asks the Fool 'Dost thou call me a fool, boy?' he gets an affirmative answer, in which even Kent seems to concur (148); and the sequence of questions reaches a frenzied climax at 223:

'Does any here know me? This is not Lear . . .
. . . Who is it that can tell me who I am?

This sequence of questions is accompanied by a series of trivial events – Lear's demand for dinner, Oswald's insolence, the knight's comment on Lear's dignity, Goneril's complaint and reduction of the retinue – each of which presses home the pathos and immediacy of Lear's impotence, so that by line 295 he is in tears. The discussions about Authority and Lear's claim to it, supported by Kent, contrast starkly with reality. Authority, in Goneril's terms, is shown to be a matter of brute force, not the immanent reality described by Kent. Thus Lear's very being, so deeply identified with his power, is brought into question at once when that power is renounced. Kent is both right and wrong.

The lack of contact becoming apparent in I, 4, is made explicit in I, 5. Lear constantly interrupts his bantering conversation with the Fool to mutter furious reflections on his daughters. Appropriately, it is in this scene that he has his first intimations of madness (I, 5, 43–4). 'I will forget my nature' (I, 5, 31) he says in an ambiguous and prophetic phrase, which may make us wonder what that 'nature' is. I, 5 marks the beginning of Lear's period of self-examination. Lear cannot be said to engage in deep self-analysis – he has been too much a man of action ever to have had time or disposition for reflectiveness. Indeed, it is just his inability to *act* effectively that he finds so painful at first. And encroaching madness is, among other things, a sign that Lear is unable to accommodate naturally the reflectiveness so brutally forced on him by his own folly. Madness even takes the place of reflectiveness, to a degree: while it fatally weakens the organism, its violent suffering exposes and purges the sufferer. In I, 5 the process is only beginning. While the Fool chatters, Lear perceives his folly and characteristically resolves to act on his insight: 'To take't again, perforce' (I, 5, 37), a resolution which shows how little he still understands his situation.

The first half of Act II is concerned with the sub-plot. We meet Lear again in Scene 4 when, finding Kent in the stocks, he is still in the dark about his own drastically lowered status, believing that: 'They durst not do't . . .' (II, 4, 21). Having quarrelled with Goneril in Act I, he now discovers the perfidy of his other daughter. In a scene filled with references to rage, temper, fire and fury we may remember Goneril's reference to Lear's 'choleric years' in I, 1, 298 and find that Cornwall is described by Gloucester in terms suggesting a parody of Lear:

You know the fiery quality of the Duke;
How unremovable and fix'd he is
In his own course. (II, 4, 88–91)

Not only is the king being punished by weapons of his own creating, Goneril and Regan, who reflect his more vicious qualities of temper; in Cornwall and Edmund he meets enemies who reflect but far surpass his arbitrary violence. For Lear, like

Gloucester, is not a saintly man, and his sufferings are, in some degree, a punishment from the gods he himself invokes. As Regan rightly says:

> to wilful men,
> The injuries that they themselves procure
> Must be their schoolmasters. (II, 4, 300–2)

Much of the tragedy's power stems from the very visible manner in which Lear brings it on himself. In this sense Regan and Goneril (who echoes her sister at II, 4, 289) act not as characters, but like the Furies in Greek drama, instruments of divine vengeance. Their patronizing cruelty sustains and deepens Lear's humiliation as, inch by inch, he is brought to a realization of his condition. In a famous and magnificent speech near the end of the scene, he reveals his state of mind, torn between the need for patience and the desire for revenge (II, 4, 262–84). The contradiction between lines 269: 'You heavens give me that patience, patience I need' and line 277: 'I will have such revenges on you both' taken together with the breaks in the thought at 268, 278, 281 and 284, indicate the depth of his distraction. What begins as a magnificient invocation to the plenitude of Nature ends in drivelling, signalling the onset of Lear's descent into real madness.

In Act III, Scene 2, the style of Lear's speeches changes to hysterical invective, as he challenges the storm. These lines (1–59) are characteristic of the language apparently approved of by Elizabethan audiences, and which we find spoken by all Marlowe's tragic heroes, for example: florid and bombastic, in the grandest heroic manner. With his usual skill, Shakespeare adapts the style to Lear's frenzy, for which it makes the perfect vehicle, juxtaposing it with the apparent nonsense of the Fool. Nowhere else in the play does Lear return to this style. It marks the high point of his rage, soon to be dissipated in madness; and this high point corresponds with the fiercest onset of the storm. The storm is central to the play, both literally and dramatically: the first half of the action works towards it, and the second half reverberates with it. Kent, who often takes a choral role in the play, supplies the comment that there has never been such a tumult (III, 2, 45–8), and the inevitable connections are made between the chaos in Lear's mind and disturbances of the natural order. This is one of several ways in which the play seeks to universalize its theme, transforming the drama from a local difficulty in a primitive heathen kingdom into an event of cosmic significance.

An important aspect of this universalizing process is the treatment of justice, a major theme of the play which Lear himself makes explicit in III, 2, 49–60. The notion of justice, both human and divine, is associated with the development of tragedy from its earliest origins in Greece. The tragic pattern presumes a natural order which is disturbed in the person of the hero, and this disturbance is echoed in the world the play presents. Shakespeare is at one with the Greek dramatists in this. When the natural order is violated – as it is by Lear's treatment of Cordelia and renunciation of his authority – universal injustice is the result, and the hero's suffering is one of the prices which has to be paid. Lear is not only the victim of disorder: he is also its source. III, 2, 49–60 shows him beginning to see the importance of justice, but not yet understanding its application to himself.

> I am a man
> More sinn'd against than sinning.

he says, which may be true if we compare his offences with Regan's or Goneril's, but fails to penetrate to the deeper truth he glimpses later in the play. When, for example, he says in III, 4:

> I have ta'en
> Too little care of this . . . (32–3)

he is beginning to see how much his kingly state has hidden from him. This is another step on Lear's way to the probing of identity, as he exposes himself to the sufferings of common men. Thus his speculations on the nature of justice are intimately connected with self-exploration.

Act III, Scene 6 covers the first period of Lear's most spectacular madness, framed as it is by the Fool's word-play and Edgar's pretended craziness. Lear stages the trial of Regan and Goneril, giving dramatic substance to the play's meditations on justice, but this is the prelude to sleep, after which he does not reappear until his encounter with the blind Gloucester in Act IV, Scene 6, when the play's two plots are brought together. This extraordinary scene, which begins with Gloucester's imagined suicide, shows both the king and the earl reaching some kind of insight, one in sanity, the other in madness. Gloucester, restored to some faith in the benevolence of the gods, resolves on patience; but as so often happens in this play, that resolve is immediately followed by something beyond imagination, in this case the entry of the mad, dishevelled Lear, covered in wild flowers. The flowers symbolize the distance Lear has travelled from his remote royal status to a kind of intimacy, albeit crazed, with the natural world where he tests his humanity. Lear's first words:

No, they cannot touch me for coining; I am the king
himself . . . Nature's above art in that respect. (83–6)

immediately introduce the identity theme in a complex irony. Like Kent earlier, Lear is both right and wrong: he is still Lear but, having renounced the crown, no longer king. And on a deeper level, his suffering may be said to have changed him into a different man: he is no longer the person who rejected Cordelia. Now he sees how he was flattered: 'To say 'ay' and 'no' to everything that I said . . .' (99); and realizes his own frailty and mortality: 'tis a lie: I am not ague-proof' (105).

Paradoxically, his words have only the semblance of madness: on examination they add up to formidable sense. When he says in response to Gloucester's question: 'Ay, every inch a king . . .' (107) these words, too, take on an ironic ring, for he immediately launches into an impassioned indictment of female promiscuity. The association of ideas here is complex but clear. Unaware of Edmund's treachery, Lear compares his supposed loyalty to Gloucester, though a bastard, with the cruelty of the king's legitimate daughters – a comparison which seems to show the natural order flouted: filial love being that order's first principle. But in Lear's clouded mind, this comparison combines with a denunciation of women implicitly associated with his hatred of Goneril and Regan. Women are seen as disruptive and destructive by virtue of the lust which rules their lives, and Lear sees only that he has suffered at the hands of two women. Goneril and Regan are therefore guilty both as women and as disloyal, though legitimate, children. In these lines Lear does not call Cordelia to mind; that only comes with his recovery. Yet if we see Lear in this speech as putting the blame for disorder on women – which has been a male habit, at least since the book of Genesis – he soon redresses the balance in his second great speech of the scene at lines 154–71, in which he combines the themes of authority, justice, lechery and hypocrisy. If woman is a whore, man is a lecher.

The imagery here occupies the familiar Shakespearian territory of appearance and reality: the powerful are those who appear to be so. Having renounced his crown at the play's outset, Lear has now discovered the true significance of his act, which has exposed him to the stresses of human existence for which the storm is so telling a symbol. What he is now renouncing are his illusions. As if to emphasize the extent of his journey towards the bare essentials of life, he turns twice in his next words to the imagery of childhood: the vulnerable, naked baby who comes crying into this world:

Thou know'st the first time that we smell the air
We wawl and cry . . . (IV, 6, 177–8)
When we are born, we cry that we are come
To this great stage of fools . . . (IV, 6, 180–81)

Bit by bit, Lear has stripped off the paraphernalia of life: honours, powers, expectations and illusions. When he wakes in Act IV, Scene 7, to find himself with Cordelia, and believing he is dead, the question must be: what is left? For the king himself, very little: 'You do me wrong to take me out o' th' grave' (IV, 7, 45). He cannot even 'swear these are my hands' (IV, 7, 55). And at long last he has come to a just estimate of himself, fittingly expressed in the plainest language, infinitely more moving than all his kingly grandeur:

I am a very foolish fond old man,
Fourscore and upward, not an hour more nor less. (IV, 7, 60–61)

It is in the apt placing of such simplicities that Shakespeare shows his supreme genius as a dramatist, for of course these words have all the force of the play's action behind them. At last Lear sees himself as he is *and* as others see him: his character and his role become the same.

The play might end at this point, but Lear's tragic progress is not yet done. The king repeats that 'I am old and foolish' (IV, 7, 84) and the act ends with ominous exchanges between Kent and a gentleman about the battle to come. When the battle is lost, Cordelia and Lear are taken, but the profound changes wrought in his condition show in his passive, even happy acceptance of necessity. This moment of coming to terms with what must be is a feature of all Shakespeare's tragedies in different forms – bitter for Coriolanus and Macbeth, stoical for Othello, calm for Hamlet. It is striking that Lear accepts his fate so joyously, only to make the contrast with what is to follow so agonizing. In the king's own words

Upon such sacrifices, my Cordelia,
The Gods themselves throw incense. (V, 3, 19–20)

Lear's final appearance is carefully managed after the long excursion in which Edmund reveals his plot and repents: it is all the more powerful because he has been forgotten by the characters – but not perhaps by the audience. In his final speech, having apparently stripped away all the extraneous layers from his life, Lear confronts death with a brief meditation on the very basis of life itself as a physical phenomenon, looking intently for the slightest sign of breath in Cordelia. It is a point of critical dispute whether his last words suggest that he believes she lives.

The development of Lear's madness

I,4   Either his notion weakens . . .
> O Lear, Lear, Lear!
> Beat at this gate, that let thy folly in, [*Striking his head.*]
> And thy dear judgment out!

I,5   O! let me not be mad, not mad, sweet heaven;
> Keep me in temper; I would not be mad!

II,4   *Hysteria passio*! down.
> O me! my heart, my rising heart! but, down!
> > O sides! you are too tough;
> Will you yet hold?
> You Heavens, give me that patience, patience I need!

III,2   My wits begin to turn.

III,4 His wits begin t' unsettle.
> Thou say'st the king grows mad . . .

III,6 All the power of his wits have given way to his impatience.
> *Fool:* Prithee, Nuncle, tell me whether a madman be a gentleman or a yeoman?
> *Lear:* A king, a king!
> His wits are gone.

The trial scene shows Lear's mind quite deranged.

IV,2 A father, and a gracious aged man
> . . . have you madded.

IV,4 As mad as the vex'd sea; singing aloud;
> Crown'd with rank fumiter . . .

IV,6 I am cut to th' brains.
> O! matter and impertinency mix'd;
> Reason in madness.

IV,7 Still, still, far wide.
> And, to deal plainly.

I fear I am not in my perfect mind.
                              The great rage,
You see, is kill'd in him.

Cordelia

        I cannot heave
My heart into my mouth.

Shakespeare was evidently intrigued by the relationship between a young girl and an older man – usually her father. Cordelia is one of a series of such girls: Desdemona (*Othello*), Imogen (*Cymbeline*), Perdita (*The Winter's Tale*), Miranda (*The Tempest*), Marina (*Pericles*), all belonging to the last phase of his career. The detailed outline of these relationships varies from play to play – in the case of *Othello*, for example, man and girl are husband and wife – but the general significance is clear: in each case the man undergoes tragic or potentially tragic experiences, but is given hope or even saved by the purity and loving trust of the girl, who embodies truth, goodness and beauty. In *Othello* and *King Lear*, Desdemona and Cordelia participate in the final tragedy as victims, and the audience's complex response to the drama is shaped as much by the heroine as by the hero. In each case a striking contrast is presented between the experienced folly of the male protagonist and the innocent wisdom of the girl. It is difficult to say a great deal about Cordelia as a character. We learn in Act V, Scene 3 from the distracted Lear that

                Her voice was ever soft,
Gentle and low . . . (271–2)

but nothing more about her person is revealed. Her pride – strong enough to match Lear's own – is evident in I, 1, and she shows courage throughout. Her leading characteristic, however, is filial tenderness. In spite of firmly informing her father that

        I shall never marry like my sisters,
To love my father all . . . (I, 1, 102–3)

it is nevertheless her visible role in the play to do just that – so much so, that the king of France is sent back to his own country by Shakespeare, leaving the field free for Lear and Cordelia at the end of the play.

Concentration on one characteristic reduces Cordelia's importance as a character and increases her dramatic and symbolic significance. If, for example, we ask ourselves whether, in the play's first scene, she should not have humoured her father's craving for flattery and reassurance, thus averting the catastrophe, we cannot answer the question in terms of character. Instead we need to look both at the play's nature and Cordelia's place in it. One might, of course, argue that whatever Cordelia does, Goneril and Regan will find a way to scheme for larger shares and come to blows, but that is hardly the point: we must deal with the play as it is, not as it might be. *King Lear* comes at the stage of Shakespeare's career when a writer who was always as much a poet as a dramatist, working in an age with a strong taste for allegory, masque and metaphor, was moving further towards the creation of a symbolic drama. This was not an even development, and in no way excluded, for example, psychological realism: the last plays contain sharply-observed portraits of all kinds. But it does mean that the last part of his career is more self-consciously preoccupied with the examination of philosophic ideas in symbolic terms. Thus individual characters, for example, are often – though not always – less important than what they represent.

This is true of Cordelia. While an actress may bring an immense amount to the part, filling it out at the beginning in a way which makes us expectant for her return, thus keeping Cordelia in the audience's mind throughout, despite her absence from the stage, it is the character's place in the play's overall structure which counts most. What is that place? It functions on a number of different levels: realistic, tragic, thematic, symbolic. On the realistic level she is the agent who precipitates the action by refusing to flatter her father. This forces him to live with his other daughters and so begin his troubles. We can accept this in terms of ordinary psychology: two equally wilful characters, who know perfectly well that they love one another most, refuse to give in to each other. In this sense Cordelia is no more virtuous than anyone else, and it would be a mistake to see her as self-sacrificing. On the contrary, it is what she refuses to sacrifice, namely the truth as she sees it, which partly causes the row. But her refusal to pander to Lear's foolishness cannot be separated from that foolishness; one is the product of the other, part of the complex of relationships within the play. While this can be seen in realistic terms as a reflection of relationships in life, by virtue of the concentration on certain elements within it – the two opposed wills, the demand for love and the insistence that love and justice cannot be separated – it also constitutes the basis of the tragic pattern, and its fundamental irony: that Cordelia's intransigence is both the cause of her father's catastrophe (though not the entire cause) and his salvation. If we see Cordelia's firmness as an inheritance from her father, who has degenerated into stubbornness, we cannot finally distinguish the play as a realistic presentation of a father's relationship with his children from its metaphysical status as a tragedy.

The thematic and symbolic levels of the play are equally involved with the others. When Cordelia reminds her father that even – or perhaps especially – between parents and children, affection's bond (she uses the word at I, 1, 92) means the recognition of natural justice

Sure I shall never marry like my sisters,
To love my father all ... (I, 1, 102–3)

she initiates her consistent association in the play with positive notions of justice, charity and mercy, themes which Lear debates with himself so passionately in Acts III and IV. But themes of the play are not only discussed, of course: they are more potently enacted. Cordelia's ability both to leave her father in Act I and to forgive him in Act IV become more than personal deeds: they express a philosophical view related to one of the play's main ideas of Nature. Cordelia is associated with the *lex naturalis*, the notion of Nature as a divine order in which everything participates, but which can be disrupted by human acts such as Lear's abdication and ill-treatment of his youngest daughter. And this philosophical notion leads us in turn to the symbolic level of the play, at which Cordelia can be seen as the representation of *caritas*(love) which is both just and forgiving in the Christian ideal. Whether we wish to go further and interpret the play in Christian terms, is a matter of taste: but even without that we can see the drama as a religious one in which Cordelia plays a vital part, and this adds yet another level to the play. *King Lear* is full of references to the gods, the heavens, the stars, divine intervention and devilish cruelty. Cordelia, on the other hand, is a human figure – pitifully mortal, as the play's end demonstrates – yet she is often associated with godly imagery. The gentleman speaks to Kent of 'The holy water from her heavenly eyes' (IV, 3, 30) and the waking Lear calls her 'a soul in bliss' (IV, 7, 46) claiming after their capture that

Upon such sacrifices, my Cordelia,
The Gods themselves throw incense. (V, 3, 20–21)

In the end, though, what Cordelia symbolizes and embodies is human virtue. The inscrutable other world to which the play constantly refers may, as Kent says, be its source: 'The stars above us govern our conditions' (IV, 3, 33) – but as the play's savagery shows, that other world does not sustain it. This makes Cordelia's goodness all the finer.

More remarkable still is the very limited scope she has for displaying it, speaking only just over 100 lines and appearing in four out of the twenty-six scenes – a demonstration of the fact that, in drama, exposure and importance are not at all the same thing. Part of the reason for such brevity lies in the difficulty of representing goodness, and this also has to do with the way in which Cordelia is less rounded in character and more symbolic in function. Shakespeare avoids the danger of priggishness or stiffness in Cordelia's character by limiting her appearances and concentrating on the later scenes in which she can be seen comforting her father. Many of her appearances in the play are in fact by report, in the words of others. Only in the first scene of the play is she exposed, and it is there we get a clue to her rare appearances and indeed, through that, to her very nature. For Cordelia is a woman of few words and – until she tries to rescue her father – fewer actions. Those are left to Goneril and Regan. Her point is simply to be – to be what she is and nothing more. Symbolically and dramatically this can best be expressed by silence – yet silence on the stage, especially in a play so overflowing with the richness of language, is a paradox. Her silence is a necessary part of her truthfulness, the very demonstration of her goodness, yet it sparks off the trouble. In other words, in the character of Cordelia the good and evil of the play touch at its very heart. When at the end Lear says 'Look on her, look, her lips . . .' (V, 3, 309) it is for the audience as though, in her death, he points to the inmost nature of Cordelia's life, and the deepest mystery of his own tragedy, in the inextricable nature of good and evil.

Gloucester

I stumbled when I saw

Gloucester can be seen as a weak reflection of Lear. The parallel between their situations is obvious: both are elderly fathers who misunderstand their children and suffer accordingly. Gloucester's personal qualities also somewhat resemble his master's: quick to suspect neglect, he is arbitrary and violent, inclined to vanity, unreflective and credulous. But Gloucester has attributes which Lear does not have. At I, 2, 100 onwards he is shown to be superstitious in a way Edmund makes fun of, and he is far less inclined than his master to look for a fight: II, 4, 117 finds him placating Lear, and in III, 3 he tells Edmund to be discreet and act secretly.

The very first scene of Act I makes the differences clear. Although, in Shakespeare's terms, Lear enters relatively soon after the play's beginning, we nevertheless meet Gloucester first. After telling us that Lear used to prefer Albany to Cornwall but now values the two dukes equally – which incidentally shows that the king has had better judgement in his time – Gloucester turns to a lewd discussion of Edmund's origins in front of his son. While this can be seen as typical courtly chit-chat, it does not show Gloucester in a good light – a point which becomes clear at the end of the play when Edgar refers to Edmund's conception as the sin which caused Gloucester's blinding:

The dark and vicious place where thee he got
Cost him his eyes . . . (V, 3, 171–2)

In the long perspective of the whole play Gloucester is placed in a severe moral context, which may be muted but not dismissed by our fundamental sympathy for him. Gloucester's fatuous joviality about the episode is not endearing, and it is sharply contrasted with Lear's solemn dignity (I, 1, 33–85). Gloucester is then overshadowed by Kent's sturdy honesty which shows him up, by implication, as a courtier, too ready to follow his master's will; and this is followed in I, 2 by his readiness to abandon Edgar and believe Edmund's plot. The first cause of this readiness is dramatic necessity: Shakespeare needs to move quickly at this point. But the effect, when taken with Gloucester's superstition (I, 2, 100–14) is to present him as feeble and – like Lear – possibly senile. As the action proceeds, the contrast with Kent is constantly brought to mind.

This effect is not so important as it may seem at first. For one thing, the scenes between Edmund and his father take on a quality of black comedy from the bastard's savage mockery and easy mastery over Gloucester. More important, the first part of the play is essentially concerned with Lear's predicament, which diverts attention from Gloucester. More important still, it is vital to the strength of the old man's change of heart in III, 3 that he should, until then, be identified with the party of Regan and Cornwall. As he admits himself, his eyes are finally opened by the blinding scene, and this takes much of its horror from unexpectedness and the innocuousness of its victim. It is from III, 3 that Gloucester's importance grows, and the sub-plot begins more faithfully to mark the plot.

In Act III, Scene 4 Gloucester confesses his grief to Kent, saying 'I am almost mad myself . . .' (III, 4, 163) a phrase in which 'almost' is the crucial word. For it is important that Gloucester does not go mad: instead he has to look the horrors of his life squarely in the face and be tempted by suicide, a means of escape he rejects after its apparent miraculous failure. Beside Lear's strength, Gloucester's uncertainty takes on added pathos. It is partly through Gloucester that we see Lear as the positively heroic figure Gloucester is not. In suffering Gloucester acquires stoicism while Lear manifests tragic grandeur, the king's responses being more extreme in proportion to his nature. The difference between the two in this sense is dramatic not moral, a matter of the effect on the audience, not of the play's value system.

Yet in the end the two – dramatic effect and moral value – cannot be distinguished. This becomes clear in the play's most violent incident: Gloucester's blinding, which synchronizes the physical horror of the act with the old man's discovery of the truth about Edmund and Edgar. The vital point about the blinding is that it takes place on stage, bringing the play's violence unavoidably into the audience's view. Even in a play full of misery and violent death, there is something exceptionally horrific about this mutilation, prepared for as it is by dozens of references to eyes, building up to Gloucester's own anticipatory lines:

Because I would not see
Thy cruel nails pluck out his poor old eyes . . . (III, 7, 54–5)

The incident's horror transforms Gloucester's moral status, changing him from an amiable temporiser into a man of moral substance, a victim of Fortune's cruelty we must take seriously. The audience is shocked into this seriousness, just as Gloucester himself is.

Just before he is blinded Gloucester expresses a belief in divine justice:

I shall see
The winged vengeance overtake such children . . . (III, 7, 63–4)

Besides the obvious and horrible irony of this remark, it takes importance from being the first in a series of reflections on divine justice which mirror Gloucester's changing state of mind. Immediately after the act, Gloucester calls upon the Gods, and when he hears the truth about his sons, says: 'Kind Gods, forgive me that, and prosper him!' (III, 7, 90). The 'Kind' is not entirely ironic: Gloucester means them to be kind to Edgar. But in the next scene, after meeting the unrecognized Edgar, he asserts that:

As flies to wanton boys, are we to th'Gods;
They kill us for their sport. (IV, 1, 36–7)

This does not necessarily contradict the notion of divine justice, but it does make it seem a matter of incomprehensible caprice – almost worse than deliberate malevolence. Yet at the end of the scene, Gloucester again changes the emphasis:

Here, take this purse, thou whom the heav'ns' plagues
Have humbled to all strokes: that I am wretched
Makes thee the happier . . . (IV, 1, 63–5)

This is an ironic echo of Edgar's own lines at III, 6, 100–108, made doubly ironic by the fact Gloucester only means that he must give Edgar money to lead him because he is blind. We, like Edgar, experience the pain of knowing Gloucester is wrong: his father's grief is his. Yet as the following lines show, Gloucester has learnt from his horrific experience: 'So distribution should undo excess' (IV, 1, 69) he tells Edgar, condemning those who will not see because they cannot feel. Earlier Gloucester had made the play's blindness/insight imagery explicit: 'I stumbled when I saw' (IV, 1, 19). Here he takes that further. In terms of his own experience – and thus all the more vividly – he expresses the truth. The fact that we have witnessed the blinding itself a few minutes earlier, helps to bring home this truth to us. The cruel truth Edgar himself expresses at V, 3, 171–2: 'The dark and vicious place where thee he got/Cost him his eyes' is something Gloucester is coming to terms with himself. When Gloucester saw the world he did not see the truth. Once he is blinded, he begins to understand:

Oh! dear son Edgar
. . . Might I but live to see thee in my touch,
I'd say I had eyes again. (IV, 1, 21–4)

In IV, 6 Gloucester thinks he is trying to commit suicide. Before doing so, he prays to the Gods. It is a prayer of acceptance. When Edgar plays his trick, convincing his father that he has been saved by divine intercession, Gloucester resolves to bear all in a speech echoing Edgar's own words at IV, 1, 25–8:

henceforth I'll bear
Affliction till it do cry out itself
'Enough, enough,' and die. (IV, 6, 75–7)

This is not his final word. After his tragi-comic meeting with the mad Lear, Gloucester prays:

You ever-gentle Gods, take my breath from me:
Let not my worser spirit tempt me again
To die before you please! (IV, 6, 214–6)

Here he combines a revived desire for suicide with submission to the gods. It is all too much to bear. But in a play about bearing, in which the central model is Job, he must bear more, and both times he gives way. The first time, after the battle is lost, he is revived in spirit by his son:

　　　　　　　Men must endure
Their going hence, even as their coming hither:
Ripeness is all. Come on. (V, 2, 9–11)

The second time, as narrated by Edgar (V, 3, 180–98) he dies of 'joy and grief'. Gloucester, like Lear, is pulled apart by his children; more exactly, by his misjudgements of them which, when rectified, still exert power because they originate in the character's very nature. They are the occasion, not the cause of the catastrophe.

The Fool

Lear's shadow

The Fool enters only in Scene 4 when the first signs of Lear's troubles are appearing. We have just heard from the knight about the disrespect shown by Goneril's servants, and it is the same knight who tells us that the Fool 'hath much pined away' since Cordelia left for France. This association of ideas – Cordelia's departure, the Fool's pining, Lear's ill-treatment – signifies the onset of the tragic process, in the first part of which the Fool is an essential participant.

With his very first words, apparently so trivial, the Fool apes and parodies Lear: 'Let me hire him too' (I, 4, 93) and it is his main function in the play to mirror the king – not as Lear would like to see himself, but as he is. The need for this lies in Lear's own character. We learn from Regan and Goneril in the first scene that he is not a reflective man: he has clearly been active and powerful, but not self-questioning. In this play it is the Fool who provides, for the first half, both the wall off which Lear can bounce his thoughts and a glass which, by telling him the truth, will provoke him to further examination. Traditionally, a fool is a licensed jester, permitted comic and critical remarks on those around him usually barred by convention or fear. The Fool must operate within limits determined by his amusement value; and his truth-telling activities are precarious, as Lear himself soon indicates when he says: 'Take heed, sirrah; the whip' (I, 4, 108). Despite these warnings, the Fool speaks his mind:

Lear: Dost thou call me fool, boy?
Fool: All thy other titles thou hast given away; that thou wast born with.
(I, 4, 145–7)

His banter is persistently concerned with the themes of Lear's foolishness, playing with the obvious pun on the word 'fool' and his own status.

The Fool is preoccupied with Lear's folly in giving his crown to his daughters, recognizing their nature more clearly than his master does. His grief at Cordelia's departure suggests that he has been close to her – a hint taken up at the very end of the play when Lear says over Cordelia's body: 'And my poor *fool* is hang'd!' (V, 3, 304). He is on the side of the virtuous characters in the play, remaining loyal to Lear throughout his appearances; yet he cannot himself be called a character so much as a disembodied intelligence. He plays no part in the action, is irrelevant to the plot, and merely follows in the king's wake, complaining about the weather! Because of this, his commentary, though full of common sense and worldly wisdom, is a kind of floating comic shadow of Lear's dark reflections. It is notable that the Fool leaves the play just when Edgar begins to become important, i.e. at the end of Act III, Scene 6. Until then the Fool has provided a critical way into the play for the audience: we have been able to remain detached spectators, enjoying the comedy and pitying the misfortune. The horror of Gloucester's blinding excludes all possibility of comedy from the play and Edgar, who is involved in the action, unlike the Fool, takes over his role as commentator, bringing them more nearly into the heart of the play. We cease to be mere spectators and become more involved.

Interestingly, both the Fool and Edgar are performers, in different senses. Edgar pretends to be what he is not, acting in a variety of different roles; the Fool is a professional entertainer. Both reflect on Lear. A king is a performer, someone who plays a public role. When Lear gives up this role he is forced to find out who he really is. The Fool and Edgar, through their 'performances', go through the process with him. In III, 4 Edgar assumes the role of the prattling madman. His style is sharply contrasted with Lear's anguished questions 'Is man no more than this?' (III, 4, 100) and the Fool's sharp and witty comments.

In this scene the Fool takes on a normative role, presenting the face of sanity beside the tattered spectacle of Lear and Edgar. 'This cold night will turn us all to fools and madmen' (III, 4, 77) is his mordant comment on the raving of his companions. In III, 6, the three of them act out the trial of Regan and Goneril in the farmhouse adjoining Gloucester's castle. Again, while joining in the macabre game, the Fool provides a sane voice. In this scene he only speaks seven times, yet his comedy anchors the scene firmly to a sense of reality, and gives us something by which to measure Lear's madness. It also heightens the pathos. Lear addresses both his companions as wise men:

Come, sit thou here, most learned justicer;
Thou, sapient sir, sit here, sit here . . . (III, 6, 21–2)

Ironically he is right: at this stage the Fool and the mad beggar are both saner and wiser than he is. As if to signal this, Lear's language in this scene comes close to the Fool's own, giving added intensity to its anguished questions and complaints. Lear, it seems, has become his own shadow.

Edmund

Thou, Nature, art my Goddess

Edmund is often compared with Iago in *Othello*, and the comparison is apt in certain respects. Both are ruthless, ingenious, quick-thinking villains, taking a sardonic self-conscious delight in their plotting, and viewing the world, as they think, with complete cynicism and black humour. Yet the differences between them are more important. While both are displaced and revengeful, Iago takes a sadistic pleasure in the suffering he inflicts, which for him is an end in itself. Believing himself above emotional weakness, Iago is consumed by hatred and pettiness: his irony springs from a profound self-doubt. Edmund, on the other hand, is entirely confident in his selfishness: he is not self-indulgently cruel, merely indifferent to the sufferings of others, which arise from the necessary steps on his way to power. The crucial distinction between them is shown by the ending of the two plays. Iago, captured and wounded, refuses to speak, his silence signifying non-cooperation: this most loquacious villain is suddenly stumped for words when he realizes the world will not go the way he wants. Edmund, however, shows a remarkable change of heart: moved, as he says, by his brother's description of Gloucester's death, he attempts a last-minute reprieve of Lear and Cordelia which is quite out of character; whatever Edmund does now can make no difference to his own imminent death. The presentation of Iago is consistent; the presentation of Edmund is not.

The reason for this difference lies in the different natures of the two plays. Put briefly *Othello* is a play of characters, *King Lear* a play of ideas. Shakespeare makes Edmund relent at the end because it heightens the dramatic effect, provides a reason for bringing back Lear and the dead Cordelia, and emphasizes the ultimate defeat of villainy. He can do this because Edmund in the play is as much a vehicle of certain concepts as he is a character.

In order to understand Edmund and his conceptual significance, we must first grasp the play's debate about Nature in which he plays such a vital part. In Renaissance thought there are, broadly speaking, two major meanings attached to the word – and the two can be made to correspond with moral ideas of evil and of good. In one sense Nature is simply the totality of forces in the universe, including everything from sexual desire to the movements of stars and atoms. Nature is a moral chaos in which everything must look after itself and in which the only observable pattern or meaning arises in conflict, the rising and falling of particular interests. War is the basic metaphor for this notion of Nature, and the play expresses it in images of predatory animals, sexual desire, violent physical acts and verbal excess. The other sense of the word includes the notion of a guiding power which gives sense and meaning to the universe. It claims to be superior to the first sense on a number of counts, not least that the very ideas of rising and falling, of war, ascendancy and defeat, are meaningless without some notion of order. In the first sense Nature is identifiable with Fortune – blind and capricious. In the second sense it is opposed to Fortune – orderly, structured and significant. It is important to note that in the second sense even suffering and death share in the order and meaning. In the first sense, the idea of love is meaningless.

While things are going well for him, Edmund's good fortune leads him into the error, common among successful men, of assuming that his success is intentional, self-created and therefore merited. Dismissing Gloucester's superstitious worries about the stars, he tells us that: 'I should have been that I am had the maidenliest star in the firmament twinkled on my bastardizing' (I, 2, 128–30). Yet he has already acknowledged, at the beginning of the scene, that the circumstances of his birth have given him not only the disadvantage of illegitimacy but also the advantage of being a love-child, thus echoing his father's point to Kent at I, 1, 21–2. Such children, he says:

> . . . in the lusty stealth of nature take
> More composition and fierce quality . . . (I, 2, 11–12)

Edmund thus embodies a contradiction: claiming special merit from his conception, yet disclaiming heavenly influence in human life. The implication is simple: he denies that there is either a moral or a divine order in the world, identifying himself with the first notion of Nature outlined above. In one way he shows himself as a more responsible character than his father, who tries to shuffle off his obligations by blaming everything on the stars. In another way he shows himself to be profoundly amoral and anarchic, an espouser of the doctrine that might is right. Like Goneril, Edmund has the rough courage of his convictions, and besides this, a sharp, coarse humour. And Edmund is not alone in his moral confusion. He is rather the extreme form of a tendency to which Lear himself is prone, i.e. the identification of his own success with the will of Nature. Lear and Edmund both learn a degree of acceptance at the end of the play – Lear in torment, Edmund in a fittingly laconic style: 'Tis past, and so am I' (V, 3, 163) and it is left to Edmund to point a moral in both their tales – namely the way in which they have forgotten that they are children not only of Nature but also of Fortune, of both Necessity and Chance. Referring to his defeat by Edgar, Edmund asks: 'But what art thou/That hast this fortune on me?' (V, 3, 163–4) and he makes the idea explicit when he says: 'The wheel is come full circle' (V, 3, 173). In this remark Edmund reveals his emblematic status: he is like a character out of a morality play. It is from the combination of this, with his creed as a Machiavellian villain, fit for spoils and stratagems, that his significance lies. For Lear's fate is too complex to express in six words and a formula. The king's discovery of Necessity through the workings of Chance is, after all, the substance of the play. It is Edmund's role, as it is Gloucester's in another way, to point up aspects of Lear's Calvary.

He does this in a number of ways besides the one just discussed. Edmund is a handsome, virile man, attractive to both Goneril and Regan. His sexuality is explicitly linked with his ruthlessness by Goneril when she compares him favourably with Albany:

Oh! the difference of man and man.
To thee a woman's services are due:
A fool usurps my bed. (IV, 2, 26–8)

This link associates him with the notion of desire as anarchic and disruptive – a notion taken up by Lear when he says: 'Let copulation thrive' (IV, 6, 114). For Lear children are the fruit of copulation and the source of all misery. Sexual desire and fertility are therefore bad. Yet the sexual act is also the very heart of Nature's order. Thus it can express either of the notions of nature described earlier: the chaotic and the orderly. The orderly notion is naturally associated with marriage and legitimacy. It is therefore appropriate that Edmund inspires adulterous passions. For him Goneril would even have her husband killed. In the sense that they are so indifferent to the order of things, Goneril and Edmund are not their father's children. Edmund's illegitimacy is thus the symbol of a truth more general in the play about true descent. It is significant that when Shakespeare adapted the old Leir story for his play he changed Cordelia's motivation from romantic to filial love. She is thus, as it were, kept out of the sexual arena, while Edmund and her sisters are firmly placed within it. As the play develops, the sexual motivation begins even to outstrip the political one in importance, thus sharpening the contrast of Cordelia's love for her father.

Edmund's good looks and attractiveness also link him with the appearance/reality theme – ironically, for he is not what he seems. At the very beginning of the play Kent describes him as: '. . . so proper' (I, 1, 17) and Edmund is well aware of this himself, taking it as a sign of Nature's favour:

When my dimensions are as well compact,
My mind as generous, and my shape as true,
As honest madam's issue . . . (I, 2, 7–9)

This contrasts with the grotesque disguise Edgar has to assume, again ironically: Edmund appears as himself, concealing a lie, while Edgar appears in disguise to reveal the truth. Thus both can be related to the identity theme, central to Lear's voyage of discovery. Edmund is the embodiment of Lear's claim that 'Robes and furr'd gowns hide all' (IV, 6, 163) though his unmasking also shows that the assertion is not always true.

Goneril and Regan

I am made of that self metal as my sister . . .

In a play in which character comes second to dramatic significance, Goneril and Regan are nevertheless clearly and positively
distinguished, and presented as individuals. Put simply, Goneril
is the stronger and more dynamic of the two, Regan the more
cautious and the more vindictive. This is established at the
beginning. At the end of I, 1 the two sisters have a conference in
which Goneril takes the lead. She is the eldest, and Lear had
asked her to speak first. She does so and sets the tone. Regan
follows suit: 'I am made of that self metal as my sister' (I, 1, 68).

After the exit of France and Cordelia, Regan and Goneril
assess the situation. Again, Goneril speaks first: Regan is for
caution but Goneril wants immediate action. Throughout the
play Goneril says more and says it more forcefully than her
sister. It is appropriate that the sister taking the lead in evil
should possess a ready tongue in sharp contrast to Cordelia's
determination on silence.

Later in Act I, Goneril stands up to her alarming father face to
face, and lectures him about his rowdy knights. Her bossy tone
aptly suggests their exchange of roles:

This admiration, Sir, is much o'th' savour
Of your other new pranks. (I, 4, 234–5)

Mixing frosty condemnation with threats, she treats Lear like a
small boy, and later employs the same method with her
husband:

Alb: I cannot be so partial, Goneril,
  To the great love I bear you –
Gon: Pray you, content. (I, 4, 310–13)

Regan, on the other hand, tries to avoid her father, going to
Gloucester's house to postpone the meeting, then sending out
excuses that she cannot see him. When Lear demands that
Regan and Cornwall come out to see him, Regan makes excuses
for not receiving Lear's knights: 'I am now from home, and out
of that provision . . .' (II, 4, 203) but, emboldened by Goneril's
presence, she too is severe and patronizing: 'I pray you, father,
being weak, seem so' (II, 4, 199).

Perhaps Regan's most unattractive trait, however, is a readiness to follow where others lead the way in cruelty. She is
vindictive and spiteful. When Cornwall proposes to put Kent in
the stocks till noon, Regan exclaims: 'Till noon! Till night, my

Lord; and all night too.' (II, 2, 131) and when her husband has put out one of Gloucester's eyes, Regan it is who makes the vile joke: 'One side will mock another; th'other too' (III, 7, 69). When an outraged servant challenges Cornwall over the blinding and they fight, it is Regan who stabs the man in the back. Fortunately relieved of her husband by the man she stabs, Regan plans to secure Edmund as her second husband. Suspecting Goneril of the same intention, she tries to bribe Oswald:

> I'll love thee much,
> Let me unseal the letter. (IV, 5, 21–2)

and babbles to him about her intentions (IV, 5, 28–38) – a thing Goneril would never do. Finally it is the elder sister who has the courage to commit murder and then suicide in pursuit of her aims: to the end she remains the stronger of the two.

It has often been noted that of all Shakespeare's later plays *King Lear* has the clearest division between good and bad characters. How seriously one takes this judgement depends on how the play is interpreted. Goneril and Regan are not good, yet Goneril has the virtues of strength and courage, albeit misapplied, and they are both allowed insights into Lear's character and situation, though to some extent this is dramatic convenience. Nevertheless it does tell us something about them. When at the end of I, 1 they discuss their father's character, they appear as shrewd and clear-eyed, well able to look after themselves. In contrast to Cordelia, the elder sisters are intensely worldly. Indeed, one is tempted to claim that they are far more fitted for power in a primitive society – and perhaps far more like their father when young – than is Cordelia. Goneril's dominant manner and Regan's shrewish diplomacy are better suited to politics than Cordelia's silence. To say this is, to some extent, to misread the play as a realistic drama – which it is only on one limited level, but it shows how Shakespeare uses all means to his ends: without fully developing the lesser characters, he is able to sketch them in sufficiently to create a full picture.

At other times the sisters take on a choric function – like other characters in the play, notably Kent and Edgar – commenting on the action and supplying a frame of reference for it. When Regan says:

> O!Sir, to wilful men,
> The injuries that they themselves procure
> Must be their schoolmasters . . . (II, 4, 300–303)

on one level – the realistic – she is sanctimoniously dismissing the sufferings she herself has helped to heap on her father by blaming him for claiming the rights he reserved to himself when abdicating i.e. his retinue of one hundred knights. But on another level she is stating one of the play's deepest truths, and a basic principle of tragedy: that the hero brings his suffering, in part, on himself, and that through it he acquires enlightenment. These levels might seem to be mutually exclusive: the puzzle of Shakespeare's drama is that they can both be accommodated. Regan and Goneril are not only themselves: they are voices, mouthpieces for things that need to be said in the play.

Thus, like Cordelia, they also participate in the thematic structure, their acts of cruelty and neglect signifying injustice and lack of love, except for themselves. Together with Edmund they represent the principle of self-love, the need for gratification whether politically or sexually. They both desire power, they both desire Edmund: appropriately, since he is himself the personification of unbridled 'natural' urges – though it is typical of Edmund to assume that the only natural urges are the ones he himself feels i.e. the need for dominance and sexual desire. Goneril makes a similar mistake when she dismisses her husband, Albany:

> Milk-liver'd man!
> That bear'st a cheek for blows, a head for wrongs ... (IV, 2, 50–51)

In her eyes Albany is a fool for not grabbing what he can get; he must also be a coward, since these can be the only reasons for not doing what one wants. In a play suffused with images of blindness and insight, Goneril is not immune from the pattern: her worldly acuteness blinds her to all other considerations. Least of all does she know herself; at the very end, when all is lost, she cries over the dying Edmund:

> This is practice, Gloucester ...
> thou art not vanquish'd,
> But cozen'd and beguil'd (V, 3, 150–53)

a remarkable complaint from one arch-plotter to another. Tragedy is about knowledge and ignorance, what is hidden and what is revealed. Evil is here shown to be, among other things, a form of ignorance and pettiness.

Edgar

A poor, bare, forked animal . . .

For most of the play Edgar is in disguise or concealment. Even in the first act he may be described as concealed in the sense that he is hidden from the truth: Edmund deceives him about Gloucester's attitude, and the trusting Edgar is ready to believe the lie. For the first third of the play, until he assumes his disguise, Edgar is of little importance, save as the object of Edmund's plot. It is only after Gloucester's blinding and the onset of Lear's madness that Edmund's significance becomes apparent.

In the short Act II, Scene 3 – a typical Shakespearian interpolation into the main action – Edgar is given a soliloquy in which he assumes his new identity as the mad beggar Tom o'Bedlam. The speech is as stylized as the situation is artificial:

I heard myself proclaim'd;
And by the happy hollow of a tree
Escap'd the hunt. (II, 3, 1–3)

The unlikeliness of all this smacks of the kind of melodrama Shakespeare's work displaced, yet it is entirely appropriate: in a highly self-conscious way Edgar is going to act a part. In contrast to Lear, who has no option, he is going to pretend to be mad. Following a favourite theme of Shakespeare's, he will find out the truth about himself by pretending to be someone else, and that 'someone else' will be the opposite of what Edgar actually is: a powerful earl's sane and handsome son becomes a poor, mad, grotesque beggar. Though Kent also pretends to be another, the functions of his disguise and Edgar's are very different: Kent merely becomes another version of himself, while Edgar becomes his own antithesis. Their reasons, too, are different. Kent dresses up to continue serving his master unrecognized. Edgar takes on

the basest and most poorest shape
That ever penury, in contempt of man,
Brought near to beast . . . (II, 3, 7–9)

in order to save his life.

Edgar's disguise is partly a matter of acting, partly a matter of seeming, and his close description of the beggar's appearance takes up the clothes imagery from the previous scene, which is to be so important in Lear's later speeches. His nakedness also prefigures Lear's exposure to the storm and his pity for

Poor naked wretches, wheresoe'er you are,
That bide the pelting of this pitiless storm . . . (III, 4, 28–29)

Edgar is central to the theme of exposure throughout the play: exposure of the individual to the cruel elements, and exposure of sin to the light. He it is who kills Edmund and Oswald and unmasks Goneril. This is no mere play on words, for the two kinds of exposure are linked in the play, most clearly by Lear (IV, 6, 154–71). The great hide behind their robes and riches; it seems nothing can get at them. Yet Lear's own experience shows that this is not always true, as does the justice meted out to Edmund, Goneril and Regan.

In III, 4 Edgar joins Lear, Kent and the Fool in a series of crazy exchanges for which Kent apparently supplies the only sane note, but which do have a logic of their own. The final subject of their chatter is the ultimate subject of the play: the nature of man. When Edgar describes himself, in answer to Lear's question 'What hast thou been?' (III, 4, 82) as

A serving man, proud in heart and mind . . .

echoing Kent's diatribe against Oswald (II, 2, 13–37), he deepens the resonance of the image of man as an obsequious, superficial, lecherous slave, introducing the animal and vermin imagery, so important in the play, and replacing Kent's insults with haunting phrases:

Let not the creaking of shoes nor the rustling
of silks betray thy poor heart to woman . . . (III, 4, 92–3)

Kent's speech is invective: this, for all its prose layout, is great poetry. In response to it, Lear describes man as '. . . a poor, bare, forked animal' (III, 4, 105) a good enough description of both Lear and Edgar at this stage. As so often in Shakespeare their exchanges take on a representative quality: they are discussing not only themselves, but all men. It is an essential part of Edgar's role in the play to provide occasions for such talk. His assumed madness makes him anyone – unaccommodated man.

As Lear descends further into madness, the fragmentation of Edgar's talk reflects this. During the mock trial in III, 6 he keeps up a stream of banter until he jerks us abruptly out of the fantastic world inhabited by Lear, the Fool and 'Tom' with two lines:

My tears begin to take his part so much
They mar my counterfeiting. (III, 6, 59–60).

Reminding us that Edgar is not mad but acting, these lines cast a curious light on the scene in which Lear is staging a 'scene' of his own. Shakespeare was fascinated by plays within plays and his work is full of references to acting, pretending, staging, producing etc., sometimes gratuitous but more usually put to dramatic effect themselves. This is no exception. Edgar represents the sanity of the audience within the play's madness – the sanity which is being tested by the horrors it sees, but which must remain if they are to distinguish sanity from madness within the play. But Edgar also hints at another meaning: so moved is he by Lear's distress that his tears threaten to reveal his deception, because only a sane person could feel for Lear: the mad are too wrapped up in their own world of illusion to notice the pain of others. That this is not an incidental mention is shown a few lines later, when the king has been carried off and the scene ends with a soliloquy for Edgar, in which his choric function is revealed; for Edgar is important not only as a participant but as a commentator on the progress of the action. In a sequence of rhyming couplets, which enforce the idea of his formal, objective commentary, Edgar states the moral of the scene, stepping out of the 'Tom' character:

How light and portable my pain seems now
When that which makes me bend makes the king bow. (III, 6, 106–7)

The poor quality of these lines and the banality of the sentiments are disturbing. It seems that after the magnificence of the preceding scene Shakespeare has suddenly dropped into bathos. But the lines need to be taken in context. They immediately precede the scene of Gloucester's blinding, which brings their complacence directly into question. That scene is followed by further comfortable reflections from Edgar:

The lamentable change is from the best;
The worst returns to laughter . . . (IV, 1, 5–6)

But these thoughts too are savagely cut short by the entrance of an old man leading the blinded Gloucester. The effect of this is devastating. Edgar's sanity and choric status – indicated by the worthy sayings he is given – naturally lead the audience to identify with his point of view. But Gloucester's blinding and Edgar's meeting with his father pull the comfortable carpet out from under our feet. It is a brilliant theatrical stroke, later echoed in the death of Lear and Cordelia, when it seems they have been saved at the last minute. It indicates the testing nature of this tragedy – the way in which Shakespeare pushes things as far as they will go – and points directly to Edgar's role as the figure who brings the audience most intimately into the play.

Recognizing his father, Edgar accepts the phoniness of his earlier thoughts:

And worse I may be yet; the worst is not
So long as we can say 'This is the worst.' (IV, 1, 27–8)

In opposition to his earlier banal remarks – an opposition made the clearer by the use of the same vocabulary – this is a true statement of the tragic predicament. Edgar is forced into a reappraisal of his own strategy:

Bad is the trade that must play fool to sorrow,
Ang'ring itself and others. (IV, 1, 38–9)

He decides that his disguise must now be positive not negative: he will not use it to hide himself, but to save his father:

Glo: I shall no leading need.
Edg: Give me thy arm:
Poor Tom shall lead thee. (IV, 1, 77–8)

To begin with Edgar appeared as an actor. As the play progresses he takes on more the role of stage-manager, organizing and foiling Gloucester's suicide, presiding over the meeting between the king and his father, killing Oswald, revealing Goneril's secret and Edmund's treachery by delivering the letter to Albany, killing Edmund, and finally accepting the commission to rule the state at Albany's hands. It is entirely fitting that Edgar should have the play's last words: tactically he dominates the final scene with his organization and his long speeches describing the unseen action of Gloucester's death and Kent's grief, just as Lear dominates it emotionally with his few final words. And it is given to Edgar to take up one of the main themes in his last lines, when he requires that the actors

Speak what we feel, not what we ought to say (V, 3, 323).

Albany

Albany is a well-meaning man married to a devilish wife, who, by virtue of her position and her personality, naturally takes the lead. He is a mixture of strength and weakness. The very fact that Goneril keeps him in ignorance of what is going on shows that she stands in some awe of him, though not much. He is not, like Cornwall, a willing accomplice of his wife, and the difference is marked between the dukes, as it is between the sisters.

Cornwall is the only character in the play without redeeming
characteristics — even Oswald shows loyalty, and Edmund
repents, or appears to: Cornwall is wicked and cruel.

In the first scene in which he takes any part, Albany tells Lear

My lord, I am guiltless, as I am ignorant
Of what hath moved you. (I, 4, 271–2)

He protests to Goneril, warning her that she may 'fear too far' (I,
4, 327). Goneril haughtily informs him that it is none of his
business, and keeps her own counsel — something Albany
accepts. Goneril is very much in charge. Were Albany to take a
greater interest he might keep his wife under control. His weakness and ignorance are thus culpable. Albany is the conventional, honourable man, unable to see problems until too late.
When one of Lear's knights comments on 'a great abatement of
kindness' and claims that it 'appears as well in the general
dependants as in the Duke himself also' (I, 4, 58–9) we can only
suppose Albany to be following Goneril's lead, persuaded by the
true argument that Lear is indeed irrational and perhaps senile.
Albany, like Gloucester, prefers peace to strife.

When Albany next appears he seems a 'man so chang'd' (IV,
2, 3). The reality of the sisters' natures has dawned on him. At
first he is almost distracted 'He smil'd at it' (IV, 2, 5) but rouses
himself, horrified at the cruelty inflicted on Lear and Gloucester. Like Edgar, he acts more wisely in the middle of the play
than at the beginning. However, he still vacillates, alternately
wondering what to do for the best and blaming himself. He will
fight the invading army because it is an invading army, but he
will not penalize Lear and Cordelia (V, 1, 25–7).

As Act V progresses Albany's strengths emerge: precisely
because he *is* conventional and honourable, he does not quail
when duty must be done, even to arraigning his wife as a traitor.
To begin with he takes a new firmness with Edmund, who is
inclined to take the lead, first telling him to be patient then
putting him firmly in his place and sardonically putting down his
wife. Twice Goneril had referred to her husband as a milk-sop –
once diplomatically and once contemptuously – now she finds
him firm in opposition, as she panics:

Shut your mouth, dame,
Or with this paper shall I stople it. (V, 3, 153–4)

At the end of the play Albany is the one figure of authority left
to clear up the mess. He seems to have learnt little from the
catastrophe, sharing out the power of the state between Edgar

and Kent, in a way which suggests he doesn't understand the problems of political division, and the symbolic significance it has as contradiction of the 'natural' order. This is hardly surprising. Albany's function in the play is not to understand but to be a kind of barometer for instinctive conventional opinion, unable to reason about wickedness, but eventually recognizing it. His ordinariness provides a standard for recognizing the unnatural or extraordinary behaviour of Lear, Cordelia, Regan, Goneril, Edmund and Cornwall. Albany is a normative character, corresponding to our expectations of average behaviour.

Kent

A very honest-hearted fellow

The appearance of Kent and Gloucester together at the beginning of the play does more than pave the way for Lear's entrance. It presents us at once with a contrast between the witty courtier, Gloucester, and the plain-spoken man Kent. This is of more than usual significance in a scene concerned with the conflict between eloquence and truth, between what is spoken and what is felt. All the characters in the play have conceptual significance, but Kent in particular becomes emblematic of a certain view, namely that plain speaking is a major virtue. This is contrasted with Cordelia's belief that at times it is better to say nothing, with Gloucester's notion that difficulties can be talked away, and with Edmund's misuse of language to get what he wants by foul means. All the characters in the play, in fact, are involved in its examination of the relationship between being and communication, and none more so than Kent.

In his conversation with Gloucester, Kent exemplifies what he is later to claim about his plain speech: all his remarks are brief and pithy in contrast to Gloucester's laboured wit. When Lear begins to make a fool of himself over Cordelia, only Kent rushes in to speak up for her and give a clear view of the king's behaviour: 'be Kent unmannerly/When Lear is mad. What would'st thou do, old man?' (I, 1, 144–5). These lines are in deliberate contrast to the flowery period Kent begins before he is interrupted by the king and they show up Kent's quick temper and refusal to suffer fools. His plainness is as much a matter of temperament as Gloucester's ornateness – more so, perhaps, because it shows most when he is least in control of himself. Kent uses the flowery style as an ironic weapon when he addresses Cornwall thus:

Under th' allowance of your great aspect,
Whose influence, like the wreath of radiant fire
On flick'ring Phoebus' front . . . (II, 2, 103–5)

Well might the duke ask what he means by it. Cornwall has just offered his own explanation of Kent's behaviour:

This is some fellow,
Who, having been prais'd for bluntness, doth affect
A saucy roughness, and constrains the garb
Quite from his nature . . . (II, 2, 92–5)

Kent, in other words, is just as false in his assumption of plainness as other people are in their courtly politeness according to Cornwall – more so, because he is making a special show of honesty other people do not claim. And it is true that Kent is needlessly provocative. He has just tried to bully the slimy Oswald into a fight, to no particular end but gratification of his own bad temper. Without accepting Cornwall's point about extra dishonesty, we may agree that such plainness is not necessarily what it seems – a point made implicitly by Cordelia, who declines to elaborate on her feelings beyond the simple statement of the position at I, 1, 94–103. The implication is clear: a vaunted plainness can be as troublesome and misleading as excessive oratorical flourishes. In I, 1 Kent only exacerbates the situation. Ironically, he is as rash and fiery as the evil Cornwall: both are distorted reflections of Lear's own obstinate temperament.

After Kent's banishment, he returns in disguise, and this associates him with the play's exploration of identity. It is ironic in the first place that one who believes so firmly in showing his true face should be forced into such deception: naturally enough he takes on the character of a gruff serving-man in a typical speech:

I do profess to be no less than I seem . . . to love
him that is honest; to converse with him that is wise
and says little . . . (I, 4, 13–16)

When Oswald appears, within a few lines, Kent loses his self-control and aristocratic arrogance replaces his plain manner. Meeting Oswald again in II, 2, he trounces him – in the process showing an unlikely mastery of invective, which reveals that Kent is not so much a man of few words as a man of his own words, and his own idea of justice. His disguise is merely another form of himself.

At the end of the play Kent remains what he was at the

beginning, and the contrast with his master's alteration is striking. Reflecting an aspect of Lear – his strength and stubbornness – Kent has not the king's scope for development. His disguise is just that, where the king's madness is a cloak underneath which he changes. Characteristically, all the secondary figures in a Shakespearian tragedy point to the protagonist, and Kent is no exception, telling us something about the king through what does *not* happen to him. Kent is unchanging, Lear is transformed. Kent, like Albany, embodies the normative world of the play by which we can measure the development of the hero. Whereas, even in disguise, Kent always remains 'himself' and knows what that self is: 'A very honest-hearted fellow, and as poor as the king' (I, 4, 19).

Structure

The play's structure is dependent on Shakespeare's adaptation of the tragic pattern to a drama of parental and filial love. The sequence of events in which a noble man falls from prosperity to adversity, recognizes his fault and thus induces catharsis in the audience, is initiated and sustained by the examination of this love, its mistakes and its lack. Lear's tragic fault is to mistake the appearance for the reality, to demand professions of love from his daughters when, as he admits, he has the substance in Cordelia. Central to the beginning of tragedy is ignorance – the hero's ignorance of a crucial fact, in this case the true nature of his daughters and – more profoundly – of himself. This is all made clear in the first scene, in which Lear's ignorance is shadowed and prefigured by Gloucester's, in the conversation between him and Kent which begins the play. Both Lear and Gloucester suffer from excessive self-love or, more precisely, self-approbation. Gloucester boasts to Kent about the promiscuity which produced Edmund; Lear counts himself wise in dividing the kingdom.

From this moment on we can interpret the structure in terms of the critical moments at which the relationships between parents and children are made clear e.g. Lear's rejection of Cordelia (I, 1, 261), his rejection by Goneril (I, 4, 290) and then by Regan (II, 4, 300), his trial of the two (III, 6, 20–76), and his repentance (IV,7,60). One might trace a similar pattern for Gloucester. Yet in terms of the structure of the play such analysis would be hopelessly incomplete. For the magnificence of Shakespeare's work – and the difficulty in discussing it – arise from the demand it seems to make that we take it on a number of levels at once, so that, whichever way we interpret the structure, it cannot be meaningfully distinguished from other things in the play. This means that the structure of *events* must be seen in the context of the conceptual and poetic structure if it is to make any sense. I have already suggested a connection between the nominal subject of the play – parental and filial love – and its tragic form. We must look for a moment at how these other elements relate to them.

Fundamental to the play, and used for articulating the different outlooks of the characters, are the different meanings of the word 'nature', which can be roughly divided into two groups. In the first, to which Edmund, Regan, Goneril, Cornwall and Oswald subscribe

– though only Edmund does so consciously – the dominant notion is what one might call survival of the fittest. There is no order, divine or human, only will-power. At the beginning of the play Lear himself tacitly subscribes to this view, identifying his royal authority entirely with his personal whim. Until driven beyond endurance, Gloucester, too, is inclined to submit to it as a way of keeping the peace: he accepts the arbitrary behaviour of Regan and Cornwall and hopes to smooth it over. Nature, as embodied in the behaviour of all these people, is simply the totality of what happens.

The second group of meanings, most clearly observable in Cordelia, is dominated by the idea of order – the notion that there is a hierarchy and a meaning in nature which can be embodied in the laws and conventions of human life and which finds its highest expression in that life. If the first group of meanings has to do with discord and conflict, this group implies the possibility of harmony achieved through love. The paradigmatic, harmonious and 'natural' loving relationship is that of parent and child, creator and created. Both groups of meanings in the play use the metaphor of sexuality – the one in terms of lechery, lust, conflict, illegitimacy, adultery and power, the other in terms of marriage, love, respect, fertility and legitimacy. The fact that both views can use the same central image shows how closely bound up they are together.

It is not possible to say that these two groups of meanings correspond straightforwardly either with the play's moral pattern or with its structure. Notions of order and harmony are certainly not borne out obviously at the end, for example. On the other hand, we can observe that Lear's tragic progress takes him through the horrors of disorder and conflict, in which he is obsessed by injustice and lechery, to a sense of loving submission and a little self-knowledge. More crudely, Edgar points the moral of Gloucester's disorder in early life when he tells Edmund that:

The dark and vicious place where thee he got
Cost him his eyes . . . (V, 3, 171–2)

Edgar sees this in terms of simple justice, but like many of his earlier generalizations (see the character sketch of Edgar) this is brought into question by the play's ending and Cordelia's cruel death.

In short, the structure of the play is complicated by the fact that its tragic form, thematic development, and the realistic drama on which these are based, do not run parallel or point to one obvious conclusion. Because structure must be seen in terms of total effect

— we must look at both ends of the bridge to observe its structure — it is not possible to talk about the structure of *King Lear* as though it were a simple and identifiable thing. There are several structures, which do a good deal to contradict one another. This is one source of the play's enormous power. It does not mean, however, that we cannot talk about structure in *King Lear* at all — only that we really need to talk about related if not always comparable *structures*.

I would like to identify three types of structure in the play. First and most obviously there are the structures of the plot. Already, as I have suggested in my discussion of them, we find differences and contradictions essential to the play's meaning (see *Plot* and the discussion of *Sources*). The table given below lists the similarities and parallels.

Plot structure

Main plot

I,1 Lear takes a sudden hatred to a beloved daughter and attaches himself to two worthless ones, owing to a weakness in his character. A momentary impulse outweighs years of affection. From this error, and its attendant circumstances, spring the calamities that befall him.

Sub-plot

I,2 Gloucester takes a sudden hatred to a beloved son and attaches himself to a worthless one, owing to a weakness in his character, and from this error spring the calamities that befall him. The reasons for Edmund's jealousy are plain from Gloucester's nonchalant introduction of him in a short conversation at the start of **I,1**.

Edmund tells Gloucester that he has often heard Edgar 'maintain it to be fit that, sons at perfect age, and fathers declin'd, the father should be as ward to the son, and the son manage his revenue', which is just what Lear has arranged in his kingdom (except that he was going to be as ward to his daughters), and the king's action makes his son's villainy more believable — 'This villain of mine comes under the prediction; there's son against father: the King falls from bias of nature; there's father against child.'

Kent banished.

II,1 Edgar banished.

II,1 Lear's servant (the banished Kent) insulted at Gloucester's castle, and Gloucester pleads for him.

4 Lear leaves Gloucester's castle and the doors are locked against him.

III,4 Lear's real madness is made worse by coming into contact with Edgar, who only feigns madness. Hazlitt draws attention to the distinction between the two, while the resemblance in the cause of their distress keeps up a unity of interest.

4 Lear will consent to go into the farmhouse only if Edgar goes too.

In disguise the banished Kent helps Lear.

III,7 Cornwall's death comes by reason of his cruelty to Gloucester.

IV,2 Goneril makes a confession of love for Edmund, but soon afterwards hears that Regan is a widow and hence is free to marry him.

5 The rivalry of Goneril and Regan for Edmund's love becomes apparent and ultimately results in the death of both of them.

III,3 Gloucester's sympathy for Lear, communicated to Edmund, leads to his blindness. Sympathy for his father's blindness lends vigour to Edgar's sword at the end.

III,7 Gloucester gets his eyes put out and is turned out of his own castle (in favour of Edmund) for helping Lear, his service to whom was betrayed by Edmund.

Gloucester says, 'Thou say'st the king grows mad; I'll tell thee, friend, I am almost mad myself.'

Edgar's sympathy with Lear, III,6,102–10

IV,1 Hence Edgar is near to his father when he needs help.

In disguise the banished Edgar helps Gloucester.

6 The victims of each plot meet. Gloucester can hear but not see Lear, and it is some time before Lear recognizes Gloucester.

7 Lear is cared for by Cordelia.

6 Gloucester is cared for by Edgar.

V,1 Goneril's wish to rid herself of Albany in favour of Edmund is revealed by Edgar (after he has slain Goneril's servant, Oswald).

3 Cordelia is slain by Edmund's orders. As a result Lear dies of shock.

V,3 Gloucester dies of shock at the revelation of Edgar's truth (and Edmund's treachery). Gloucester dies off the stage, as otherwise it would have made Lear's death appear an anticlimax to his.

At the end, Albany, the only survivor (except for France, in whom no one is interested) of the Lear group, confers with Edgar, the only survivor of the Gloucester group, about the welfare of the state in the years immediately ahead.

In any play there is a clash of wills or personalities; this is what 'makes' the play. Within the structure of these two parallel plots, notice the clashes:

1 Between armies of different nations.
2 Between rival groups for mastery in the same country.
3 In families.
4 Between individual characters. Character-contrast is a fundamental principle in Shakespearian drama.
5 In men's hearts and minds, e.g. Lear, when he thinks of the wrong he has done Cordelia.
6 Between puny man and the strength and vastness of the physical forces of the universe (III,2).

Thematic structure

King Lear is a play especially rich in themes: ideas of nature, political and moral order, family relationships, madness, appearance and reality, love and death – all the great themes of human discourse, in fact – are covered in the play. I have already suggested one way of looking at this structure in the discussion of Nature. Associated with notions of Nature are the different ideas of love we find in the play, which range from Oswald's contemptible self-seeking loyalty, to Cordelia's devotion to her father. If we look at the play in terms of this theme we can see a clear enough sequence:

(1) Gloucester's declaration of his affection for Edmund.
   Lear's preference of Regan and Goneril over Cordelia.

(2) Edmund's declaration of self-love and betrayal of Edgar and his father.
Goneril's rejection of her father, followed by Regan's.
(3) Edgar's love for Gloucester, in spite of his father's unjust treatment.
Cordelia's love for Lear in spite of his.
(4) Goneril and Regan both lust after Edmund.
(5) Reconciled with Edgar, Gloucester dies of 'joy and grief' in conflict.
Reconciled with Cordelia, Lear dies of joy and grief in conflict.
(6) Edmund and Regan are killed, Goneril kills herself.
Albany, Edgar and Kent survive.

The crucial point in this sequence is 3. One might say that whereas the *plot* climaxes in the last act, when its strands are drawn together, the love theme reaches its high point when Edgar and Cordelia both show their readiness to forgive the wrongs their fathers have inflicted on them. In Edgar's case we see this happening in IV, 1. In Cordelia's case we hear about it in IV, 3. Between these two scenes, in IV, 2, we get the first hint of a conflict between Goneril and Regan over Edgar:

Gon: But being widow, and my Gloucester with her,
May all the building in my fancy pluck
Upon my hateful life . . . (IV, 2, 84–6)

Goneril's possessive 'my Gloucester' indicates what is to come. This is only resolved in the play's last scene, where it might appear that all the parties, loving and hating alike, suffer equally. What counts here is the values which have been established for the audience. Cordelia, Lear, Gloucester die in both grief and joy; Edmund, Goneril and Regan are entirely frustrated. The good is shown to be precarious but it does exist. Love is its own reward as indeed Cordelia points out in I, 1, 92:

I love your majesty
According to my bond; no more nor less.

This is a gentle rebuke to Lear, who wants to have the cake of love and eat its flattery. Even at the end he does not quite understand the impossibility of this: 'Have I caught thee?' (V, 3, 21) he asks, with tragic irony, still wanting somehow to possess Cordelia, as he once thought he 'possessed' his kingdom. But love and possession are opposites, as Lear has to learn. This is the meaning of the gradual stripping away of one layer after another of his life, which characterizes another aspect of the play's structure, insofar as that is identical with a close examination of the king. First authority, then its trappings, then sanity, then clothes themselves, then any vestige of dignity – all go, and Lear ends as a lowly, broken prisoner, a pathetic dribbling old man, howling over the corpse of his daughter. This bitter ending brings the theme of love itself into question. Now Lear can only die and become part of that 'nothing' which has resounded through the play. When everything we think we possess has been stripped away, what is left?

Linguistic structure

The third structural aspect I would like to distinguish is the linguistic one. This cannot, of course, be separated ultimately from the themes – or even from the plot: everything in the play is made of words. But the plot might be articulated in different ways, the themes given different emphasis, the characters differently related. And precisely because a play is made of words – even the action can only be deduced from them – it is vital to have some idea of what sort of words they are.

The major Shakespearian tragedies have clearly distinguished linguistic and stylistic identities related to their natures. The erotic and exotic elements of *Antony and Cleopatra*, for example, are reflected in the richness of the imagery. *Hamlet* has an enormous richness of vocabulary, suiting its sophisticated, cosmopolitan manner. *Othello* is filled with paradoxes and oxymorons which reflect the central contradiction of the marriage between Desdemona and Othello. *King Lear*, as the most symbolic and even allegorical of these tragedies, appropriately seems to have the plainest language, reserving its brighter colours for Lear himself and for the mad scenes – though even there the verbal shading is largely a matter of proper names. It is dramatically appropriate that the king should have the finest words, if not the best: he is the protagonist and the character on whom most of our attention is concentrated.

Lear has a variety of styles within the play which indicate his emotional, moral and mental state. His first entrance is grand and royal and his first speech is grave, formal and measured, as are his responses to Regan and Goneril. When he finds Cordelia resisting him, the hint of a new manner emerges: Lear remains majestic, but his quick temper and violent disposition show through. The scene is ceremonial, with disturbing undercurrents. Goneril and Regan, by their change of manner from public to private, reveal how they humour the king and conceal from him their real views. Kent establishes his reputation for plain-speaking, while showing himself capable of the flowery speech which is to get him into trouble with Cornwall. But the plainest speaker is Cordelia, and with her utterances Shakespeare introduces into the play a theme which fascinated him through life: the contradiction between what is inexpressible – in her case, love – and the necessity of expressing it. This reminds us that Shakespeare was not only acutely sensitive to the qualities of language: he was also aware of the philosophical problems associated with it, one of which is embodied in the first scene's contrast between the eloquent but unfaithful elder sisters, and the quiet but true Cordelia.

When we meet Lear again (I,4) he has put off his regal manner and is speaking prose. Only when Goneril enters and enrages him does Lear turn again to verse, and the hints of instability from the first scene are taken up. The sentences are brief, even broken. It is in Scene 4 of Act I that Lear begins his great sequence of speeches meditating on the themes of ingratitude, justice, loyalty and authority. These are magnificent, but in a very different style from I, 1. Here the magnificence is the sign of frantic, impotent, hysterical rage – not of authority, but of servitude. Words do not merely express: they also compensate for weakness. This becomes painfully apparent in III, 2 as he combats and challenges the storm. We can measure the progress he makes during Acts II, IV and V by comparing any of the speeches in III, 2 with the plainness of his words to Cordelia when he wakes from sleep:

I am a very foolish fond old man,
Fourscore and upward, not an hour more or less (IV, 7, 60–61)

The king has, as it were, come round to his daughter's own plainness of speech and simplicity of sentiment, having in the scenes preceding this one reached the height of his madness and the height of eloquence.

There is a complex issue here. The play's sanity is represented by different kinds of plain speech: Kent's, Cordelia's, Albany's, Edgar's. Yet some of its deepest insights come in the apparent craziness and inconsequence of Lear's madness, Edgar's feigned madness and the Fool's banter. Humour and irony in Regan, Goneril and Edmund are associated with evil. The Fool's wit, and the black comedy of the mad scenes, are associated with goodness. There is, in other words, no direct correlation between any one style and any one moral or intellectual level. What counts is the dramatic context – yet this does not always override philosophical considerations – such as those which associate Cordelia's simplicity and dignity with depth and truth of feeling. There can be reason in madness, just as there is a kind of madness in the apparent reason of Edmund, Regan and Goneril. And in Edgar's case, there can even be reason in feigned madness – a reason which discovers itself through the feigning of that madness. Just as we cannot make simple statements about the structure, so the style too has its complexities, of necessity in such an immensely complex play.

At the end of the play Lear returns to a highly-coloured style for the shocking revelation of Cordelia's body. What strikes one about this last appearance, though, is the range of style, from the ranting

Howl, howl, howl!O! you are men of stones . . . (V, 3, 256)

through the matter-of-factness of

This is a dull sight. Are you not Kent? (V, 3, 281)

to the ecstasy of

Do you see this? Look on her, look, her lips,
Look there, look there! (V, 3, 309–10)

In each case the vocabulary is simple; 90% of the words are monosyllables. One famous line is composed of the same dissyllable repeated: 'Never,never,never,never,never!' (V, 3, 307) echoing an earlier line of Lear's: 'Then kill,kill,kill,kill,kill,kill!' (IV, 6, 185). These repetitions, which represent the ultimate simplification of language before silence itself, both show Lear faced with emotions so unbearable that they go beyond the possibility of syntax or the construction of coherent sentences. They are cries of unhelpable despair.

But they are not just cries. The two words Lear finds in his choking misery – kill and never – are both final words and they offer one key to the linguistic pattern of the play. *King Lear* is a play of extremes: love and hatred, cruelty and nobility, madness and cold reason, age, climate, nakedness – are all present in excess. At the heart of the play is a very old, temporarily very mad king. All the other tragedies have heroes in the prime of life. Lear's own extremity – his smouldering life which is so close to death – sets the tone in a way we can observe in the language. Take the word 'nothing' for example. It first occurs in I, 1.

Lear: Speak.
Cord: Nothing, my lord.
Lear: Nothing?
Cord: Nothing.
Lear: Nothing will come of nothing: speak again.

Repeated, like 'never' in the last act, five times, the word at first has a purely dramatic quality, embodying Lear's disbelief that Cordelia can mean what she says. He picks up her bare repetition and turns it into a truism. He means that if she says nothing she will get nothing. There, for the time being, we may leave it, merely noting Lear's echo at I, 1, 244. We might tie the word in with the many references to value, price, worth etc in the first scene and deduce that Cordelia is now nothing to Lear – and possibly also that Lear is now the king of nothing: he has given his substance away.

When Edmund tells Gloucester in I, 2 that the letter he is reading is 'nothing' we probably don't connect that use of the word with Lear's in Scene 1. But when Gloucester tells Edmund that his betrayal of Edgar will lose him nothing (I, 2, 112) we might begin to wonder. Gloucester will reward Edmund for his falseness as Regan and Goneril were rewarded for theirs. And the strong echoes begin in I, 4 when Kent tells the Fool his song is nothing:

Fool: Can you make no use of nothing, Nuncle?
Lear: Why no, boy; nothing can be made out of nothing.

The Fool implies that Lear has made himself nothing by giving away his land, referring to him a few lines later as: '. . . an O without a figure . . .' (I, 4, 189) and telling him explicitly: '. . . thou art nothing . . .' (I, 4, 191). These lines immediately precede Goneril's entrance to berate her father and so cause his first serious spasm of self-questioning. The word is thus associated with the theme of identity. This is the light in which it next appears, in Edgar's soliloquy, when he decides to assume disguise. His last words: 'Edgar I nothing am', play on two senses: 'I'm no longer Edgar' and 'if I stay as Edgar, I'll be caught and killed'. This pun, uniting the notions of changed identity and death, points to one of the play's leading ideas. King Lear has already died as a king and been reborn as a man. But he dies twice more, in madness and bodily, each time with a different identity. Before he learns the lessons of nothingness Lear is still disposed to attribute it to others. Furious with Goneril, he tells Regan that 'Thy sister's naught . . .' (II, 4, 131) and when the two sisters join forces to deprive him of his knights, he cries 'I gave you all' (II, 4, 248). It is after this that the storm and Lear's madness begin and Lear enters on the purgatory which questions his repeated claim: for he is forced to discover whether nothing can be made of the nothing he has become.

By itself, the word 'nothing' has no force: it takes its power from the context, associated as its usage is with a whole string of ideas and images, all of which revolve round the notion of identity in the form of two questions: Who am I? and What is a human being? The first question is directly discussed by Lear, the second arises from the action and language of the play. The animal imagery, for example, which is pervasive, constantly prompts us to think about the differences and similarities between men and other creatures. The imagery of disguise brings personal identity into question – especially when, paradoxically, it is the disguise of nakedness which both Lear (III, 4, 107) and Edgar (II, 3) adopt – though in Lear's case it is a 'disguise' which takes him a step nearer to the nothingness of the end.

The imagery of sight and blindness underlines and elaborates on the identity theme. Gloucester, with whom the image is most vividly associated, is a man who, like Lear, has failed to see the reality of his own nature. Not until he is physically blinded does he achieve moral insight:

I stumbled when I saw. Full oft 'tis seen,
Our means secure us, and our mere defects
Prove our commodities. (IV, 1, 19–21)

Linking the sight/blindness image here with another preoccupation of the play – the superfluity of means which prevents us from true understanding – Gloucester cries out for forgiveness from Edgar – the son who is standing a few feet away. In this one ironic moment his predicament is summed up. The moment is prepared. From Goneril's first claim that she loves her father more than 'eyesight, space and liberty' (I, 1, 55) images of sight and blindness recur again and again. In the same scene Lear orders Kent 'Out of my sight!' and Kent replies: 'See better, Lear; and let me still remain/The true blank of thine eye' (I, 1, 157–8). Cordelia disclaims a 'still-soliciting eye' (I, 1, 230) as she does a lying tongue; and refers to the 'wash'd eyes' (I, 1, 267) with which she leaves her father. The implications of all this, set in context, are that Cordelia has true insight, while her father is deceived by appearances. Gloucester too is taken in by Edmund, who shows him a forged letter and later stages a scene of mimic fighting with Edgar so that his father will 'see' the truth with his own eyes.

When shown the letter Gloucester says, with anticipatory irony: 'Let's see: come; if it be nothing, I shall not need spectacles' (I, 2, 35) and Edmund replies, with equal irony: 'I find it not fit for your o'er-looking' (I, 2, 38). Edmund is right, Gloucester wrong. This sequence of images continues through the play until the scene in which its significance is made explicit, IV, 1. Gloucester meets his son unknowingly, but says that last night he saw a man who reminded him of Edgar, but that now he has 'heard more' (IV, 1, 35) – a painful reminder of his condition. But Gloucester is stoical and points the moral of his own tale, describing himself as one of those 'that will not see/Because he does not feel' (IV, 1, 67). Because he did not see he did not understand. Because he did not feel he did not see. Now he cannot see he has learnt to feel and begun to understand. He repeats his earlier idea that 'the super-fluous and lust-dieted man' (IV, 1, 66) is the least perceptive. This is, in fact, an enunciation of the tragic doctrine that suffering produces insight. Gloucester is, as it were, drawing the map for our understanding of Lear – and that is the general function of the imagery: to give substance and subtlety to the dramatic framework, which is meaningless without it.

General questions plus questions on related topics for coursework/examinations on the books you may be studying

1 Discuss Edmund's role in the play.
Suggested notes for essay answer:

Edmund is brave, intelligent, daring, quick-thinking, unself-pitying, cruel, cold, ruthless and selfish. There is an emblematic quality to much of his part i.e. he emerges more as a representative villain than as an individual.

After briefly appearing with Gloucester in I,1 his role is firmly established by the soliloquy in I, 2, which shows him as both sardonic and humorous. Edmund is supremely self-confident because he doesn't care about anything. At the end of the play he faces death without qualms. He has had his throw and lost the game.

He is shown to be paradoxical: on the one hand he believes in the blind forces of nature – life as a ruthless game in which the strongest win. On the other hand he thinks of himself as autonomous and in control of his own life. Edmund is sharply contrasted with his brother Edgar, and with Cordelia. He is identified with Goneril and Regan as an unfaithful child. The play's opening establishes Edmund's paternity, but he rejects it.

He is the chief instrument in bringing Gloucester to catastrophe, and he also contributes to Lear's death, by spurring on Goneril and Regan, and by having Cordelia killed.

Edmund is a focal point of the play's irony. Betraying Edgar with a letter, for example, he is himself betrayed by Goneril's letter to him. Sardonic about his brother, he is eventually destroyed by him.

The following points need to be taken into account:

a) Edmund's illegitimacy, announced at the play's beginning. The contrast with Edgar's legitimacy, and Gloucester's attitude to them both in this respect.

The way in which this is related to 'true' and 'false' children themes in the play e.g. the contrasts and comparisons with Regan, Goneril and Cordelia.

The extension of the notion of illegitimacy to political, moral and emotional levels of the play e.g. the various attempts to usurp power and property, to commit adultery, and to go against 'natural' emotions of filial love.

b) Edmund's handsomeness, also mentioned by Kent near the beginning of the play.
How this relates to the appearance and reality theme: Edmund is not what he seems. Sharp contrast with Cordelia.
The way in which charm and good looks make Edmund feel he is naturally destined for the good things of life.
The part his sexual attractiveness plays in the plot, intensifying the rivalry between Goneril and Regan.

c) Edmund's Machiavellianism.
This is expressed philosophically in the play as a view of Nature in which ruthless self-seeking is the approved and inevitable way of going about things.
Edmund is a skilful and daring plotter, caught out by his own stratagems. He rejoices in his own wickedness, and is a focus for the play's many predatory animal images. He puts power before everything.

d) Edmund's acknowledgement of Fortune's role at the end. He has put Chance above Necessity, and perished by chance. He sees the world as a place in which everything is up for 'grabs'.

2 What is gained by bringing the Gloucester story into *King Lear*? Show how Shakespeare interweaves the two stories, setting down all the points of contact between the two.

3 Describe the part played by letters in *King Lear*.

4 Discuss the importance of the storm scenes in *King Lear*.

5
Regan: 'Tis the infirmity of his age: yet he hath ever but slenderly known himself.
Goneril: The best and soundest of his time hath been but rash.

Is this dialogue an adequate clue to Lear's character?

6 Do you agree that Lear was 'more sinn'd against than sinning'?

7 Comment on the suggestion that the play of *King Lear* might well be called 'The Redemption of Lear'.

8 How far is King Lear a characteristic Shakespearian tragic hero?

9 To what extent do you consider Cordelia responsible for the tragedy of *King Lear*?

10 Compare and contrast the character of Cordelia with that of *either* Goneril *or* Regan.

11 Contrast Goneril with Regan, and Albany with Cornwall.

12 Sketch the development of Gloucester's character in the play, comparing it with the development of the character of Lear.

13
As flies to wanton boys, are we to the gods;
They kill us for their sport.
The gods are just, and of our pleasant vices
Make instruments to plague us.

Which of these quotations respresents your interpretation of *King Lear*?

14 Edmund says of his own ending, 'The wheel is come full circle'. How far is this also true of the fate of Lear, Gloucester and Cordelia?

15
               This is some fellow,
Who . . .   . . . doth affect
A saucy roughness, and constrains the garb
Quite from his nature: he cannot flatter, he,
An honest mind and plain, he must speak truth!

How far do you consider this a correct and sufficient estimate of the character of Kent?

16 'This is not altogether fool, my lord.' Discuss the dramatic function of the Fool in the light of this remark.

17 In the popular eighteenth-century version *King Lear* was given a happy ending, in which Lear was restored to his kingdom and Edgar was married to Cordelia. Say what you think of Shakespeare's ending contrasted with this one.

18 'The language of poetry is metaphor.' Do you agree with this? Give your reasons, with illustrations from *King Lear*.

19 Mention any features of *King Lear* that were conditioned by the theatre for which Shakespeare wrote.

20 Write an account of a leading character in any play or novel you have read for whom life changes as a result of his/her decisions.

21 Bring out clearly the theme of loyalty or disloyalty in any book you are studying.

22 Discuss the part played by family relationships in any play you have seen or read.

23 Compare the presentation of the violence in *King Lear* with that in any other book you know well.

24 Compare King Lear with any character of major importance in any other Shakespeare play.

25 Examine the images used by any other author and say what they contribute to your appreciation of his or her work.

26 Write an appreciation of a poem you have read which deals either with a storm or extreme weather conditions or a natural disaster.

27 Write a dialogue between two or three people who are having an argument, bringing out the reasons for their disagreement.

28 'Old age is sad.' By looking at one or two situations in any book you have read, say whether you agree or disagree with this statement.

29 Write about a character or characters who appear to be mad in any book you have studied.

30 Give an account of any book you have read where there is very little humour, saying whether or not you enjoyed reading it.

Further reading

There is an enormous literature concerning *King Lear*. Below are listed a few of the more accessible recent publications.

The Arden Shakespeare: King Lear, edited by Kenneth Muir (Methuen, 1972)

Shakespeare: King Lear, N. Brooke (Edward Arnold). A close study of the text. Very helpful for relating the two plots to the structure.

Shakespeare's Doctrine of Nature, J. F. Danby (Faber). Idiosyncratic and contentious but illuminating on *King Lear* as a play of ideas.

King Lear, ed. F. Kermode (Casebook Series, Macmillan). A useful selection of essays with an excellent introduction.

King Lear in our Time, M. Mack (Methuen). A survey of different interpretations with a personal view. Well-written and stimulating.

Aspects of King Lear, ed. Muir and Wells (CUP). Includes helpful essays on language and a survey of recent views.

The Wheel of Fire, G. Wilson Knight (UP). Contains the classic exposition of the play as a dramatic poem.

The Great Stage, R. B. Heilman (University of Washington Press). An excellent detailed study of the imagery and themes.

Prefaces to Shakespeare, H. Granville-Barker (Batsford). Shows in detail how the play works on the stage.